THE COLLECTED POEMS OF
WILFRED OWEN

W9-AYQ-033

THE
COLLECTED POEMS
OF
WILFRED OWEN

*Edited with an Introduction
and Notes by*

C. DAY LEWIS

and with a Memoir by
EDMUND BLUNDEN

A NEW DIRECTIONS BOOK

Library of Congress Catalog Card No. 64–10290
Copyright © Chatto & Windus Ltd, 1963

Poems by Wilfred Owen, with an Introduction by Sieg-
fried Sassoon, was first published in 1920 and reprinted
in 1921. A new edition, with notices of his life and work
by Edmund Blunden, was first published in 1931, and
reprinted in 1933 (with corrections), 1946, 1949, 1951, 1955,
1960, 1961 and 1963. This amended edition first published
in the United States in 1964. First published as
New Directions Paperbook 210 (ISBN: 0-8112-0132-5) in 1965.

New Directions Books are published for James Laughlin
by New Directions Publishing Corporation,
80 Eighth Avenue, New York 10011

Manufactured in the United States of America
New Directions Books are printed on acid-free paper.

NINTEENTH PRINTING

CONTENTS

Other Poems, and Fragments

Minor Poems, and Juvenilia

ACKNOWLEDGEMENTS

I WOULD like to thank the poet's brother, Harold Owen; his cousin, Leslie Gunston; Sir Osbert Sitwell; Siegfried Sassoon, and the British Museum authorities, for making available to me the drafts of the poems in their possession.

To Harold Owen I am deeply grateful also for allowing me to see the letters written by Wilfred to his family, for the many informative talks I have had with him about his brother, and for the encouragement and practical help he has given me.

I owe a special debt to Dr. D. S. R. Welland, who generously put at my disposal his unrivalled knowledge of the Owen texts: his suggestions, criticisms, and careful checking of my work have been invaluable.

In common with every other reader of Owen's poetry, I am indebted to Siegfried Sassoon and Edmund Blunden, whose devoted editing of the poems, in their editions of 1920 and 1931, did so much for Owen's fame and has so considerably lightened the task of the present editor. I am grateful to Edmund Blunden also for allowing me to reprint, with a few minor alterations, the Memoir he wrote for the 1931 edition.

C.D.L.

MAIN DATES OF WILFRED OWEN'S LIFE

March 18, 1893

Born, at Plas Wilmot, Oswestry, Shropshire, in the house of his maternal grandfather, Edward Shaw. The Owen family remained here till 1897.

1895

Birth of Mary Owen.

1897

Birth of Harold Owen. The family had moved to Shrewsbury in the spring of this year. After about a year, the Owens moved again—to Birkenhead.

1900

Birth of Colin Owen.

April 30, 1900

Wilfred Owen registered for entry into the Birkenhead Institute. He joined the school on June 11 of this year, and remained there until 1907, when the family returned to Shrewsbury.

1907

Owen began attending the Shrewsbury Technical School as a day boy.

September 1911

Matriculated at London University.

October 1911 to summer 1913

At Dunsden vicarage, Oxfordshire, as pupil and lay assistant to the Reverend Herbert Wigan.

c. August 1913

Obtained post as tutor in English at the Berlitz School of Languages, Bordeaux. Took up the post in September.

c. July 1914

Left Berlitz School, became tutor to two boys in a Catholic family in Bordeaux.

c. September 1915
Returned to England.

October 22, 1915
Joined the Artists' Rifles.

June 4, 1916
Commissioned in Manchester Regiment.

c. December 29, 1916
Sailed to France on active service, attached to Lancashire Fusiliers.

March 19, 1917
Sent to 13th Casualty Clearing Station. Owen returned to his battalion early in April: on May 1 or 2 he was again sent to the 13th Casualty Clearing Station, and from there to the 41st Stationary Hospital. In June he went into No. 1 General Hospital, from which he was returned to England, arriving at the Welsh Hospital, Netley, about June 18.

June 26, 1917
Transferred to Craiglockhart War Hospital, Edinburgh.

November 1917
Discharged from Craiglockhart: posted to Northern Cavalry Barracks, Scarborough.

August 31 or September 1, 1918
Returned to France for active service.

October 1, 1918
Awarded Military Cross.

November 4, 1918
Killed in action, trying to get his men across the Sambre Canal.

INTRODUCTION

WILFRED Owen must remain, in one respect at least, an enigma. His war poems, a body of work composed between January 1917, when he was first sent to the Western Front, and November 1918, when he was killed, seem to me certainly the finest written by any English poet of the First War and probably the greatest poems about war in our literature. His fame was posthumous—he had only four poems published in his lifetime. The bulk of his best work was written or finished during a period of intense creative activity, from August 1917 (in one week of October he wrote six poems) to September 1918—a period comparable with the *annus mirabilis* of his admired Keats. The originality and force of their language, the passionate nature of the indignation and pity they express, their blending of harsh realism with a sensuousness unatrophied by the horrors from which they flowered, all these make me feel that Owen's war poems are mature poetry, and that in the best of them—as in a few which he wrote on other subjects—he showed himself a major poet.

The enigma lies in this maturity. Reading through what survives of the unpublished poetry Owen wrote before 1917, I found myself more and more amazed at the suddenness of his development from a very minor poet to something altogether larger. It was as if, during the weeks of his first tour of duty in the trenches, he came of age emotionally and spiritually. His earlier work, though an occasional line or phrase gives us a pre-echo of the run of words or tone of thought in his mature poetry, is for the most part no more promising than any other aspiring adolescent's of that period would have been. It is vague, vaporous, subjective, highly 'poetic' in a pseudo-Keatsian way, with Tennysonian and Ninety-ish echoes here and there: the verse of a youth in love with the *idea* of poetry—and in love with Love.

And then, under conditions so hideous that they might

have been expected to maim a poet rather than make him, Owen came into his own. No gradual development brought his work to maturity. It was a forced growth, a revolution in his mind which, blasting its way through all the poetic bric-à-brac, enabled him to see his subject clear—'War, and the pity of War'. The subject made the poet: the poet made poems which radically changed our attitude towards war. The front-line poets who were Owen's contemporaries—Sassoon, Rosenberg, Graves, Blunden, Osbert Sitwell—played a most honourable part, too, in showing us what modern war was really like; but it is Owen, I believe, whose poetry came home deepest to my own generation, so that we could never again think of war as anything but a vile, if necessary, evil.

* * *

Wilfred Edward Salter Owen was born at Oswestry on March 18th, 1893, of middle-class stock. His father, a man of adventurous spirit, had taken himself to India at the age of eighteen, having obtained a job with the Peninsular Railways. After four years he returned to England, married, and took a post on the railway here. But he never reconciled himself to a career which gave so little scope for enterprise and adventure.

Wilfred's mother had been brought up in a Calvinistic and rigidly 'Victorian' atmosphere. Her family had been comfortably off; but when her father died, it was found that he had lived on his capital. Throughout her married life, therefore, she had to subsist and bring up a family on her husband's salary alone. The straitened means of their parents were to affect profoundly the lives of Wilfred, his sister and his two brothers: it can also be surmised that the contrasting nature of his parents—the father's independent, impatient spirit, the mother's gentleness, conventionality and deeply religious disposition—helped to set up in Wilfred's mind that tension between opposites which so often creates the artist.

Both father and mother, though far from being intellectuals, were cultivated people. Mr. Owen was a well-informed man who kept up serious reading to the end of his life, and was not without discernment in the other arts, especially music. Mrs. Owen had shown, as a girl, considerable technical accomplishment in painting. The civilized atmosphere of the Owen home did much to compensate for the lack of those higher educational facilities which, money being so short, the parents could not give their children. Had Wilfred had the benefit of a University education, for instance, his intellectual development would have been more rapid; but his poetry would not necessarily have been the better for that.

His relationship with his mother, whose favourite he was, remained the closest one in his short life. Indeed, his letters to her* read like those of an only child, with the warmth and the touch of possessiveness which an only son so often shows towards his mother: in his adolescence, these letters tend to be 'literary'; we are aware that he is trying to impress her, just as later, writing from France, he spares her few of the horrors, appealing—though unconsciously and tacitly—for her special sympathy. Towards his sister and younger brothers Owen is very much the eldest son: he writes to them at times almost as if he were their father, with quaint touches of pontificating and lecturing relieved by a levity which is often slightly condescending. We get the impression of a serious, clever but naïf youth, a little smug, a little 'old-fashioned', who feels responsible for the younger members of his family, as might the eldest son of a widowed mother. We see, prefigured here, the sense of responsibility Owen was to feel as an officer towards his own men in France, and as a poet towards all the soldiers fighting and suffering there.

In boyhood, Wilfred Owen had many interests. He studied botany and archaeology, became a competent pianist, began to read widely, moving on from the Sherlock Holmes stories to Dickens, Scott, George Eliot and Ruskin. Years later he was to write from Craiglockhart War Hospital, "Believe me, if the letter of Ruskin is little worshipped today, his spirit is everywhere. My one grudge against that Prophet is that he warned us so feebly against the War." It has been said that Owen was no great reader. Certainly, in his letters to his mother he does not often mention books—or his own

*Unless otherwise stated, all quotations from Owen's correspondence are from letters written to his mother.

writing. But, when he died, he left a library of 325 volumes, which was not bad for a young man with very little money to spare. These included editions of many poets—Dante, Chaucer, Goethe, Southey, Gray, Collins, Cowper, Shelley, Keats, Coleridge, Burns, Browning and Tennyson, for instance; a number of French classics and text-books; nearly all Shakespeare's plays; a fair sprinkling of novels, from Jane Austen to Hardy; and miscellaneous volumes attesting to his interests outside literature. Owen's reading was at random perhaps (as a poet's often is), and undirected; but he got through a good deal of it.

At what age he began writing verse, I have not been able to determine. But the poetic temperament was fully formed by the age of eighteen. In a letter of April 2nd, 1911, he wrote "Leslie tells me you are often hearing the nightingale. Is it indeed so enchanting? I crave to hear it, and yet I should almost be afraid lest it should not be as fine as I imagine it." Some MS. notes in Harold Owen's possession, undated, but probably of this period, fill out the picture of a youth oppressed by the vague dissatisfaction and disillusionment, the morbid negativism of adolescence:

Why have so many poets courted death?

1. *Dissatisfaction when visiting some spot of literary or historical association.*
   The impossibility of seeing the departed hero. Uncertainty of changes in buildings, and landscape.
2. *Mental fatigue accompanying prolonged gazing at objects of art, paintings, sculpture.*
3. *Same with beauties of Nature—omnipotent sense of transience and temporality.*
4. *Perversity of my nature—when alone, a lovely sight makes me long for someone else to enjoy it with me: with some equisite [sic] scene or sound (nightingale) or solemn place . . . around me, a companion annoys me with lack of feeling, solemnity, sympathy (yea perception) of my emotion.*
5. *When I am reading or studying, I long to be out, up and doing. When out, on holidays, I feel time wasted and crave for a book.*

On the reverse of the folio Owen wrote,

Consummation is Consumption
We cannot consummate our bliss and not consume.
All joys are cakes and vanish in the eating.
All bliss is sugar's melting in the mouth.

Owen was not so thoroughly introverted at this age as the above notes might suggest. He could look outwards. Writing to his brother Harold, then an art student, in June, 1911, he said,

I wished you could daub some representation of a Field, which I saw blazing with yellow charlock, backed by a Beech-wood of a deep green so nearly black that it puts one in mind of the colour of an ancient black coat assuming its green old-age tints.

Such precise, and rather Hardy-esque, observation is as rare, though, in Owen's youthful letters as in his juvenilia. These early poems, glowing and grandiose like technicolour sunsets, were written in a state of infatuation. Owen had not merely fallen in love with Keats; he felt for him at once a reverence and a strong affinity. On seeing a MS. book of Keats's in the British Museum, he remarked (letter of September 17th, 1911),

His writing is rather large and slopes like mine . . . He also has my trick of not joining letters in a word . . . I seem to be strangely familiar with it.

On this characteristic of Owen, Osbert Sitwell justly observed—"He manifested a tremendous capacity for admiration, for reverence: a quality which perhaps every poet, however much of a rebel he may be in other directions, must needs possess."

*　　　*　　　*

The year 1911 marked a new departure in Owen's life. He had been a pupil at the Birkenhead Institute from 1900 to 1907, then attended the Shrewsbury Technical School. In September, 1911, he matriculated at London University. Money, however, was too short for him to be able to take up courses there. So, in October, he went to Dunsden, Oxfordshire, as a pupil and lay assistant to the vicar.

At this time, Wilfred Owen was still a Christian believer, and there seemed a possibility that he might in due course enter Holy Orders, after studying theology and practising pastoral work under the vicar. The effect of Dunsden upon him, however, was far different from what had been anticipated. The vicar, though an amicable man, does not appear to have been a very inspiring one: from Wilfred's letters home, we learn that the Reverend Herbert Wigan possessed a large number of picture frames, and used to take his pupil into Reading to buy pictures of the right size to fit them. Neither Owen's fellow pupils nor the parishioners offered him any intellectual stimulus. He wrote (letter of January 26th, 1912),

But the isolation from any whose interests are the same as mine, the constant, inevitable mixing with persons whose influence will tend in the opposite direction (away from systematic study)—*this is a serious drawback.*

But, if intellectual companionship was lacking, his work at Dunsden (for which he received £1 a month) did make one profound impression upon Owen's mind. Visiting among the rural slums of that Oxfordshire parish, he was brought up hard against certain facts of life—squalor, sickness, and a poverty far more crippling than the straitened means of his own family. This experience must have knocked holes in his introspective, subjective habit of mind, and forced him to look outwards at the real world. The tremendous force of indignant compassion which sweeps through his war poems did not have its origin in the Western Front: we feel it first in certain letters from Dunsden.

. . . a gentle little girl of five, fast sinking under Consumption—contracted after chicken-pox. Isn't it pitiable . . . the Father is permanently out of work, and the Mother I fancy half starving for the sake of four children. This, I suppose is only a typical case; *one of many* Cases! *O hard word! How it savours of rigid, frigid professionalism! How it suggests smooth and polished, formal, labelled, mechanical callousness!*

Letter of March 23rd, 1912.

They may have (e.g. the fires of revolt may have died down) *in the bosoms of the muses, but not in my breast. I am increasingly liberalising and liberating my thought . . . From what I hear straight from the tight-pursed lips of wolfish ploughmen in their cottages, I might say there is material ready for another revolution.*

Letter of April 23rd, 1912.

This awakening of a social conscience in Owen was soon followed by, if indeed it did not cause, a lapse from the Christian faith. On January 4th, 1913, in a letter to his mother, he declared,

I have murdered my false creed. If a true one exists, I shall find it. If not, adieu to the still falser creeds that hold the hearts of nearly all my fellow men.

Failure of conviction, and an illness, caused him to give up his work at Dunsden. In August of this year he obtained a post as English tutor at the Berlitz School of Languages in Bordeaux, and went out the next month to France, a country he had twice visited with his father between 1907 and 1910. He held this post until July 1914, when he became tutor to two boys in a Catholic family in the same city.

During this period Owen suffered from recurrent minor ailments—he had not been robust as a child, and the chilly damp of two Oxfordshire winters had done his health no good—the details of which he assiduously reported in his letters home. Though it enabled him to improve his French, the job provided no great interest and only a bare living wage. He became a bit of a hypochondriac: he felt discouraged about his future, and had no certain conviction as to what he should do with his talents. What *was* his vocation?

It is more like the call of an art which morning and evening makes me unhappy in my unfruitful labour. What art? . . . Any! . . . I am happy with Art. I believe in Science *more wholeheartedly than in Art, but what good could I do in that way?*

Music? If only I dare say Yes! I certainly believe I could make a better musician than many who profess to be, and are accepted as such.

. . . I love Music, Violin first, Piano next, with such strength *that I have to conceal the passion for fear it be thought weakness . . .*

My Temperament I have now no right to doubt. That I believe infallible; though it remains to know which, if any, Music, Painting, Sculpture, or Verse, is the most possible.

Letter of May 24th, 1914.

Sixteen months before this, Owen had written in an effervescent (and Keatsian) way,

For the first time in life, I feel I could fill volumes; if I once started to write. It would turn out a Philosophical Work, of course. Oh the irony of my old title of Philosopher!*. I have become one without knowing it. It is a far, far different thing from what I imagined of yore . . . My treatise on Philosophy would be a succession of interrogations from beginning to end.

Letter of January 24th, 1913.

When Owen went to live with the Leger family, things took a brighter turn. In August 1914 he was introduced to M. Laurent Tailhade—the first professional poet, so far as we know, he had ever met: the two struck up a friendship, Owen profiting by the older man's encouragement and example. Tailhade, too, had been intended for the Church, but had lost his Christian belief. With his employer, Mme. Leger, Owen was on excellent terms, their relationship having an element of light-hearted flirtatiousness: but at this time Owen was still under-developed emotionally, his idealism, and a streak of the puritan acquired, perhaps, from his mother, holding him back from closer contacts with women. In an undated letter from Bordeaux he had written, "All women, without exception, *annoy* me, and the mercenaries . . . I utterly detest." It is noticeable that, in his war poetry, Owen had no pity to spare for the suffering of

*A family nickname.

[18]

bereaved women: even *Greater Love* sees women as not quite worthy of the men who are dying in France.

His two pupils were bright, high-spirited boys who gave him no trouble. Owen evidently had a gift for getting on well with the young, and an unsentimental approach to them. A letter of January 29th, 1913, from Dunsden, shows that he thought a good deal about child psychology and education, and was well aware how strong an influence he could exercise upon young minds: "Children are not meant to be studied, but enjoyed. Only by *studying to be pleased* do we understand them." He adds later, with a prophetic foresight truer than he could have realized, "I am convinced that I hold under my tongue, powers which would shake the foundations of many a spiritual life." Certainly, his spiritual influence on poets of my own generation was very great.

*　　*　　*

When war broke out, Wilfred Owen, a provincial himself, was living the life of a cultivated, French provincial society. He was now twenty-one—unsophisticated, inexperienced, still only intermittently sure of his vocation, but ardent and sensuous at the core. For a month or two, the war hardly touched him or the social circle in which he lived. His own attitude towards it was not that of a "swimmer into cleanness leaping": it was nearer to that of certain Bloomsbury figures who resented the war as an unseemly disturbance of the private life; but with this difference—that Owen's protest was raw, violent, naïf, deadly serious:

> *I feel my own life all the more precious and more dear in the presence of this deflowering of Europe. While it is true that the guns will effect a little useful weeding, I am furious with chagrin to think that the Minds, which were to have excelled the civilization of two thousand years, are being annihilated— and bodies, the product of aeons of Natural Selection, melted down to pay for political statues.*

Letter of August 28th, 1914.

A month later, Owen was for the first time brought up hard against the facts of war. The experience, since he had a poet's inner toughness, proved salutary rather than traumatic. He visited a hospital in Bordeaux at which casualties had just arrived from the front—a hospital grievously ill prepared for such an emergency, with an inadequate water-supply, where he witnessed operations being performed without anaesthetics. In a letter of September 23 to his brother Harold, he wrote:

One poor devil had his shin-bone crushed by a gun-carriage wheel, and the doctor had to twist it about and push it like a piston to get out the pus . . . I deliberately tell you all this to educate you to the actualities of war.

The tone is ruthless and a little self-important; but Owen was a very young man, and young men do labour to educate their families. But there is a sharpness in the observation which comes like a premonition of the unrelenting factual truthfulness we find in Owen's war poems: he wanted to shock, but never for the mere sake of shocking.

In general, his letters of the Bordeaux period show a greater interest in other human beings, and a considerable talent for sketching their externals, but no deep perception of their natures, nor any desire to see deep into them. He was still egocentric, as a young poet must be; still repeating his "need for study, intellectual training"; still oscillating between confidence and self-distrust over his vocation—on the one hand, "I seem without a footing on life; but I have one . . . I was a boy when I first realized that the fullest life liveable was a Poet's" (letter of February 6th, 1915); on the other hand, "all last year and longer I have read no poetry, nor thought poetically" (letter of February 18th, 1915). At the beginning of 1915 Owen was seriously considering whether he should take up an opening in business. He seems to have had no thoughts yet of enlisting: in any case he was bound by his contract with the Legers to stay in France till the end of the summer. It was not till June 15th that he first stated his intention of joining up as soon as his tutorial engagement was over, and there is no indication in his letters home that he had felt any conflict or compunction about remaining a civilian.

He came home in August or September, was accepted for the Army in October, and trained with the Artists' Rifles. On June 4th, 1916, he was commissioned in the Manchester Regiment. His early training took place in London, where he visited the Poetry Bookshop—Harold Monro was "very struck" by some sonnets of Owen's, and "told me what was fresh and clever, and what was second-hand and banal; and what Keatsian, and what 'modern'," (letter of March 5th, 1916). Military training he found, as most 'temporary' soldiers find it, both arduous and tedious; apart from the discipline it inculcated, it was inevitably a playing-at-soldiers which could be only the sketchiest preparation for the realities of active service. In August, Owen contemplated a transfer to the Royal Flying Corps: "Flying is the only active profession I could ever continue with enthusiasm after the War." But he was too useful an infantry officer to release, and at the end of the year he received his orders to go out to France.

Little need be added to the picture of Owen's life during the next twenty-three months, which Edmund Blunden gave in his Memoir.* His first tour of duty, on the Somme sector, proved his staunchness as a man and made the fibre of his best poetry. This rapid maturing is seen not only in his verse but in his letter-writing, which loses its former doubts and affectations, and gains in honesty and eloquence. It is instructive to compare the passage quoted in Blunden's Memoir (p. 173), beginning "But chiefly I thought of the very strange look on all faces in that camp," with a passage written a year earlier, when Owen was at the Etaples transit camp on his way to the front:

> *On all the officers' faces there is a harassed look that I have never seen before, and which in England never will be seen—out of jails. The men are just as Bairnsfather has them—expressionless lumps.*

> Letter of January 4th, 1917.

For those who have no memories of the First War, two things need to be said. For the combatants on the Western

*See Appendix I.

Front it became, compared with the Second War, a static one. In every sector, its background was very much the same—a desolate landscape of trenches, craters, barbed wire, ruined buildings, splintered trees, mud, the corpses of animals and men. Writing home on February 4th, 1917, Owen described

> *the universal pervasion of* Ugliness. *Hideous landscapes, vile noises, foul language . . . everything. unnatural, broken, blasted; the distortion of the dead, whose unburiable bodies sit outside the dug-outs all day, all night, the most execrable sights on earth. In poetry we call them the most glorious.*

Yet, though this ubiquitous landscape surpassed all the imagined horrors of Dante's Inferno, it provided the soldier poets with a settled familiar background, while trench warfare gave them long periods of humdrum passivity. Such conditions—a stable background, a routine-governed outer life—have so often proved fruitful for the inner lives of poets that we may well attribute the excellence of the First-War poetry, compared with what was produced in the Second War—a war of movement—partly to the kind of existence these poets were leading: another reason could be, of course, that they were better poets.

Secondly, we shall not fully understand the poetry of protest written by Owen, Sassoon and others, unless we realize how great was the gulf between the fighting man and the civilian at home, and between the front-line soldier and the brass-hat. To the soldier, those on the other side of the barbed wire were fellow sufferers; he felt less hostility towards them than towards the men and women who were profiting by the war, sheltered from it, or wilfully ignorant of its realities. Shortly after Owen was sent for a second time out of the line—a victim of 'neurasthenia' caused, he said, by "living so long by the *disiecta membra* of a friend", he wrote (letter of May 2nd, 1917),

> *Already I have comprehended a light which will never filter into the dogma of any national church: namely that one of Christ's essential commands was, Passivity at any price! Suffer dishonour and disgrace, but never resort to arms. Be bullied, be outraged, be killed; but do not kill . . .*

Christ is literally in no man's land. There men often hear his voice. Greater love hath no man than this, that a man lay down his life—for a friend.

Is it spoken in English only and French? I do not believe so.

This was not the Christ of Owen's religious upbringing: it was the one whom David Gascoyne addressed many years later as 'Christ of Revolution and of Poetry'. He appears again in a letter Owen wrote to Osbert Sitwell on July 4th, 1918, when he was training troops in England and himself preparing to return to the front:

For 14 hours yesterday I was at work—teaching Christ to lift his cross by numbers, and how to adjust his crown; and not to imagine he thirst till after the last halt. I attended his Supper to see that there were not complaints; and inspected his feet that they should be worthy of the nails. I see to it that he is dumb, and stands at attention before his accusers. With a piece of silver I buy him every day, and with maps I make him familiar with the topography of Golgotha.

Wilfred Owen went back to the front line because he felt that there he would be in a stronger position to voice his protest against the war, and speak for his comrades. On October 4th, 1918, he wrote home about the action in which he won his Military Cross, a battle which

passed the limits of my Abhorrence. I lost all my earthly faculties, and fought like an angel . . . You will guess what has happened when I say I am now commanding the Company, and in the line had a boy lance-corporal as my Sergeant-Major. With this corporal, who stuck to me and shadowed me like your prayers, I captured a German Machine Gun and scores of prisoners . . .

My nerves are in perfect order.

A month later, to the day, he was killed.

*　　　*　　　*

What Wilfred Owen's future as a poet would have been, had he survived the war, it is impossible to say. War is the subject of nearly all his best poems, and a reference point in others, such as *Miners*. It is true that he wrote a few poems of great merit on other subjects. But when, during the great productive period, he sought to write or finish such poems, we often notice in them a regression to his immature manner. It is interesting to speculate upon what subjects might have fired his imagination and possessed his whole mind, as did the war experience. Would the vein of savage indignation prove exhausted, or might Owen have found it renewed in the struggle against social injustice which animated some of his poetic successors? It seems possible; but his honesty, fervour and sensuousness might have been directed elsewhere to produce a Catullan kind of love-poetry. My own conviction is that, whatever poetry he turned to, he would have proved himself in it a poet of a high order. His dedication was complete: he passionately wanted to survive the war, so that he might continue to write poetry.

Certainly, in the writings of his last two years, he showed himself both a serious poet and an increasingly self-critical one. If we follow the successive drafts of the poems over which he worked longest—*Anthem for Doomed Youth*, for instance*—we can see how admirably he kept sharpening the language, focusing ever more clearly his theme. Clumsiness there sometimes is, in these later poems; but nothing facile, and no shallow amateurism. Even his juvenilia, undistinguished though for the most part they are, present one promising feature—a gift for sustaining, in the sonnet form particularly, what musicians call *legato*; for keeping the movement of the verse running unbroken through an elaborate syntactical structure.

The language and rhythms of Owen's mature poetry are unmistakably his own: earlier influences have been absorbed, and we recognize in the style an achieved poetic personality. But it was achieved not solely through the impact of war: the seeds of it can be found in such early lines as

> *. . . the lie*
> *Of landscapes whereupon my windows lean*

*See Appendix 2

or

I kissed the warm live hand that held the thing

or

For us, rough knees of boys shall ache with rev'rence

or

I shall be bright with their unearthly brightening.

Although his later work was largely cleared of derivativeness and false poeticism, Owen was not a technical innovator except in one respect—his consistent use of consonantal end-rhymes (grained/ground; tall/toil). For a detailed discussion of this device, I would refer the reader to Chapter Six of D. S. R. Welland's book on Owen.* Consonantal rhyme, and other forms of assonance, are common in Welsh poetry and had been used previously in English by Vaughan, Emily Dickinson and Hopkins. There is no evidence that Owen had read any of the three last; nor could he read Welsh—his parents were both English and he was born in England. The first surviving poem in which he experiments with consonantal rhyme is *From My Diary, July 1914*, while *Has your soul sipped?* (see note, p. 113) may be another early experiment. A letter of April 10th, 1916, also shows his mind running on it: "We had Night Operations again. I was isolated scouting—felt like scooting." Dr. Welland puts up an interesting case for Owen's having been introduced to this device by the poetry of Jules Romains, a volume of which, making frequent use of *accords*, came out in 1913.† On the other hand, as Welland recognizes, Owen may well have discovered it for himself: a young poet's head is full of chiming sounds: it is a matter of nerve and skill, not necessarily of outside authority, whether he comes to use, deliberately and successfully, chimes which to orthodox ears would sound discordant.

*Wilfred Owen: a Critical Study (London: 1960).
†But no copy of Romains' work was found amongst Owen's books; and I can discover no reference to Romains in his correspondence.

Again, it has been noticed how Owen tends to have a lower-pitched vowel following a higher one as its rhyme; and this has been explained as a method of stressing the nightmare quality or the disillusionment of the experience about which he was writing. It may be so. But, lacking a theoretical statement by Owen about his rhyme, we should be cautious in attributing its workings to any *methodical* practice. Poets, when they have such urgent things to say as Owen had, seldom attend so consciously to musical detail; the harmonies of the poem, and its discords, are prompted by the meaning rather than imposed upon it. Nevertheless, Dr. Welland is justified in saying that Owen's consonantal rhyming "is right for this poetry because its note of haunting uneasiness, of frustration and melancholy, accords perfectly with the theme and the mood".

By temperament and force of circumstances, Owen had led a solitary life, cut off from any close fraternity with other men, out of touch with the cultural movements of pre-war England. Shy and diffident as he was, this previous isolation must have heightened the sense of comradeship he felt when, in the army, he found himself accepted by his fellows and able to contribute to the life of a working unit. The old solitude was fertilized by the new fraternity, to enlarge his emotional and imaginative scope. Laurent Tailhade's eloquently uttered pacifist beliefs had, no doubt, impressed themselves upon the young Owen; but I can find no evidence that Owen was influenced by his poetry. At the Craiglockhart War Hospital, Owen met a man whose poetry and pacifism appealed to him alike. Siegfried Sassoon brought out, in a way almost embarrassing to him, all the younger poet's capacity for hero-worship: he had been a most gallant Company commander; he had written poems and a prose manifesto condemning the war in an uncompromising manner. No wonder Owen felt at first like a disciple towards him.

It was a sign of Owen's integrity and growing independence as a poet that his work was not radically affected by his admiration for this new friend. In a few satirical or colloquial poems, such as *The Letter*, *The Chances*, or *The Dead Beat*, we may perceive Sassoon's influence; but Owen must have known that Sassoon's ironic and robust satire was not for him, and he continued in the tragic-elegiac vein which he had started working before he met the other poet. What Sassoon gave him was technical criticism, encouragement, and above all the sense of being recognized as an equal by one whose work he respected: it meant the end of his isolation as an artist.

In a letter from which I have already quoted, Wilfred Owen described himself as "a conscientious objector with a very seared conscience". He had come to see the war as absolutely evil in the agonies and senseless waste it caused: on the other hand, only as a combatant could he conscientiously and effectively speak for the men who were suffering from it. This conflict within himself, which Dr. Welland has discussed at length,* was a basic motive of the war poems. It is a conflict every honest poet must face under the conditions of modern total war; for, if he refuse to take any part in it, he is opting out of the human condition and thus, while obeying his moral conscience, may well be diminishing himself as a poet. This conflict is seldom overt in Owen's war poetry, which, although it makes use of his personal experiences, is remarkably objective: his 'seared conscience' and his inward responses to that experience provided a motive power, not a subject, of the poetry.

Looking once again at this poetry, thirty-five years after I first read it, I realize how much it has become part of my life and my thinking—so much so that I could hardly attempt dispassionate criticism of it. Now, as then, I find Owen's war poetry most remarkable for its range of feeling and for the striking-power of individual lines. "He's lost his colour very far from here" would stand out even in a play by Shakespeare or Webster: "Was it for this the clay grew tall?" has a Sophoclean magnificence and simplicity. Ranging from the visionary heights of *Strange Meeting* or *The Show* to the brutal, close-up realism of *Mental Cases* or *The Dead Beat*, from the acrid indignation of such poems as *Dulce Et Decorum Est* to the unsentimental pity of *Futility* or *Conscious*, and from the lyricism of *The Send-Off* to the nervous

*op. cit., Chapter Five.

dramatic energy we find in *Spring Offensive*, the war poems reveal Owen as a poet superbly equipped in technique and temperament alike. He was not afraid to be eloquent; and because he was speaking urgently for others, not for self-aggrandisement, his eloquence never ballooned into rhetoric. The war experience purged him of self-pity and poetic nostalgia. During his great productive year, the pressure of his imaginative sympathy was high and constant, creating poems that will remain momentous long after the circumstances that prompted them have become just another war in the history books. They, and the best of his poems not directly concerned with war, are in language and character all of a piece.

*   *   *

The Text

The bulk of Wilfred Owen's autograph poems are in the British Museum, to which they were presented by the Friends of the National Libraries in 1934. Other MS. drafts, and transcripts, are privately owned. My notes to the poems indicate the present whereabouts of all the drafts I have been able to trace. In the notes, I use the following abbreviations:

BM   British Museum
SS   Siegfried Sassoon, or his edition of 1920
EB   Edmund Blunden, or his edition of 1931
HO   Harold Owen, the poet's brother
LG   Leslie Gunston, the poet's cousin
OS   Sir Osbert Sitwell, Bart.

I have already paid tribute to the admirable work performed by Mr. Sassoon, Professor Blunden and Dr. Welland in tackling the textual problems set by the MS. drafts. Owen wrote a number of drafts and part-drafts of many of these poems, and it is not always possible to determine the order in which these drafts were composed. Where I have occasion to compare what we can be reasonably sure was his final draft with earlier ones, I indicate the former by *BM* (*a*), the latter by *BM* (*b*).

I have myself worked through all the available MS. material, seeking amongst the numerous deletions and

[28]

variants with which some even of the final drafts face an editor, to discover Owen's intention or to arrive at the most satisfactory text where that intention is not clear. In general, my text will not often be found to differ greatly from Blunden's, though I have made a considerable number of small emendations to his: such changes, small or great, are pointed out in the notes.

In two poems, Blunden's text differs from that in any of the extant drafts and I have been unable to trace a MS. source. The poems in question are *The Unreturning* and *It is not Death*. There can be no doubt that Professor Blunden had MS. authority for the versions he printed; but unfortunately the material he collected for his edition has been dispersed, and he is unable to help me over this matter. His version of *Shadwell Stair* gives 'lapping Thames' for the 'full Thames' which appears in the only MS. draft I can trace. In certain other poems—*Greater Love*, *Conscious*, *To My Friend*—Blunden conflated two or more MS. drafts: these, and other minor points, are mentioned in my notes.

The purpose of the notes is not to give a complete *apparatus criticus*, but chiefly to record such variants as show how Owen improved a line or a passage through successive workings, or variants which are of intrinsic interest. I have also, where possible, drawn upon his correspondence to comment upon the specific experience that went to the making of a given poem and thus fixes the date after which the poem was written.

Since it is not possible to date a great number of these poems, I have arranged them in a non-chronological order. Part One gives all the completed poems which are directly concerned with the war: first, those treating it in a more general, distanced way; then those which convey the soldier's first experiences of war; then the poems which describe action and its aftermaths. In Part Two I have placed poems on other subjects, or not primarily concerned with the war, together with some fragments. Part Three offers a selection of Owen's juvenilia and minor poems, chosen to illustrate some of the things I have said about his youthful work and sensibility.

C. Day Lewis

PREFACE

THIS book is not about heroes. English poetry is not yet fit to speak of them.

Nor is it about deeds, or lands, nor anything about glory, honour, might, majesty, dominion, or power, except War.

Above all I am not concerned with Poetry.

My subject is War, and the pity of War.

The Poetry is in the pity.

Yet these elegies are to this generation in no sense consolatory. They may be to the next. All a poet can do today is warn. That is why the true Poets must be truthful.

(If I thought the letter of this book would last, I might have used proper names; but if the spirit of it survives— survives Prussia my ambition and those names will have achieved themselves fresher fields than Flanders. . . .)

WAR POEMS

Strange Meeting

It seemed that out of battle I escaped
Down some profound dull tunnel, long since scooped
Through granites which titanic wars had groined.
Yet also there encumbered sleepers groaned,
Too fast in thought or death to be bestirred.
Then, as I probed them, one sprang up, and stared
With piteous recognition in fixed eyes,
Lifting distressful hands as if to bless.
And by his smile, I knew that sullen hall,
By his dead smile I knew we stood in Hell.
With a thousand pains that vision's face was grained;
Yet no blood reached there from the upper ground,
And no guns thumped, or down the flues made moan.
"Strange friend," I said, "here is no cause to mourn."
"None," said that other, "save the undone years,
The hopelessness. Whatever hope is yours,
Was my life also; I went hunting wild
After the wildest beauty in the world,
Which lies not calm in eyes, or braided hair,
But mocks the steady running of the hour,
And if it grieves, grieves richlier than here.
For of my glee might many men have laughed,
And of my weeping something had been left,
Which must die now. I mean the truth untold,
The pity of war, the pity war distilled.
Now men will go content with what we spoiled,
Or, discontent, boil bloody, and be spilled.
They will be swift with swiftness of the tigress.
None will break ranks, though nations trek from progress.
Courage was mine, and I had mystery,
Wisdom was mine, and I had mastery:
To miss the march of this retreating world
Into vain citadels that are not walled.
Then, when much blood had clogged their chariot-wheels,
I would go up and wash them from sweet wells,
Even with truths that lie too deep for taint.
I would have poured my spirit without stint

But not through wounds; not on the cess of war.
Foreheads of men have bled where no wounds were.
I am the enemy you killed, my friend.
I knew you in this dark: for so you frowned
Yesterday through me as you jabbed and killed.
I parried; but my hands were loath and cold.
Let us sleep now. . . ."

BM has final draft, and five drafts of a passage leading up to and including the present ll. 28–39. HO had one early draft, which he presented to the editor of this edition.

l. 10: BM (a) has *dead* deleted: also, cancelled, *Yet slumber droned all down that sullen hall*. This line is omitted by S.S.

Between ll. 13 and 14 Owen wrote and cancelled *But all was sleep. And no voice called for men.*

l. 15: EB *the other,*

l. 25: BM (a) has 'the *one thing* war distilled' altered to 'the *pity* war distilled.'

l. 39: in BM (a) this line is circled and arrowed to become the final line of the poem. *Let us sleep now* appears to have been written in later and tentatively. HO ends poem with the present penultimate line, below which Owen has written *But not in war.*

l. 40: BM (b) gives *I was a German conscript, and your friend.*

Insensibility

Happy are men who yet before they are killed
Can let their veins run cold.
Whom no compassion fleers
Or makes their feet
Sore on the alleys cobbled with their brothers.
The front line withers,
But they are troops who fade, not flowers
For poets' tearful fooling:
Men, gaps for filling:
Losses, who might have fought
Longer; but no one bothers.

II

And some cease feeling
Even themselves or for themselves.
Dullness best solves
The tease and doubt of shelling,
And Chance's strange arithmetic
Comes simpler than the reckoning of their shilling.
They keep no check on armies' decimation.

III

Happy are these who lose imagination:
They have enough to carry with ammunition.
Their spirit drags no pack,
Their old wounds, save with cold, can not more ache.
Having seen all things red,
Their eyes are rid
Of the hurt of the colour of blood for ever.
And terror's first constriction over,
Their hearts remain small-drawn.
Their senses in some scorching cautery of battle
Now long since ironed,
Can laugh among the dying, unconcerned.

IV

Happy the soldier home, with not a notion
How somewhere, every dawn, some men attack,
And many sighs are drained.
Happy the lad whose mind was never trained:
His days are worth forgetting more than not.
He sings along the march
Which we march taciturn, because of dusk,
The long, forlorn, relentless trend
From larger day to huger night.

We wise, who with a thought besmirch
Blood over all our soul,
How should we see our task
But through his blunt and lashless eyes?
Alive, he is not vital overmuch;
Dying, not mortal overmuch;
Nor sad, nor proud,
Nor curious at all.
He cannot tell
Old men's placidity from his.

But cursed are dullards whom no cannon stuns,
That they should be as stones;
Wretched are they, and mean
With paucity that never was simplicity.
By choice they made themselves immune
To pity and whatever mourns in man
Before the last sea and the hapless stars;
Whatever mourns when many leave these shores;
Whatever shares
The eternal reciprocity of tears.

BM has one draft; HO has one draft, heavily corrected.
l. 5: BM has *Dances on the hard ground* deleted.
                    Feel not
l. 8: BM has *That one should   , poetic* deleted.
l. 55: EB gives *moans*. BM has *mourns* cancelled and *moans* substituted. I prefer *mourns*, as did SS.

Apologia Pro Poemate Meo

I, too, saw God through mud,—
    The mud that cracked on cheeks when wretches smiled.
    War brought more glory to their eyes than blood,
    And gave their laughs more glee than shakes a child.

Merry it was to laugh there—
    Where death becomes absurd and life absurder.
    For power was on us as we slashed bones bare
    Not to feel sickness or remorse of murder.

I, too, have dropped off fear—
    Behind the barrage, dead as my platoon,
    And sailed my spirit surging light and clear
    Past the entanglement where hopes lay strewn;

And witnessed exultation—
    Faces that used to curse me, scowl for scowl,
    Shine and lift up with passion of oblation,
    Seraphic for an hour; though they were foul.

I have made fellowships—
    Untold of happy lovers in old song.
    For love is not the binding of fair lips
    With the soft silk of eyes that look and long,

By Joy, whose ribbon slips,—
    But wound with war's hard wire whose stakes are strong;
    Bound with the bandage of the arm that drips;
    Knit in the webbing of the rifle-thong.

I have perceived much beauty
    In the hoarse oaths that kept our courage straight;
    Heard music in the silentness of duty;
    Found peace where shell-storms spouted reddest spate.

Nevertheless, except you share
    With them in hell the sorrowful dark of hell,
    Whose world is but the trembling of a flare,
    And heaven but as the highway for a shell,

You shall not hear their mirth:
    You shall not come to think them well content
    By any jest of mine. These men are worth
    Your tears. You are not worth their merriment.

November 1917.

BM has two drafts, the earlier unfinished and entitled *Apologia pro Poema Disconsolatia Mea*. HO has three early drafts, one entitled *The Unsaid*.
l. 4: HO *And glee, that almost made the gloom worth while.*
l. 8: HO *For God forgets Christ then, and blesses murder.*

Greater Love

Red lips are not so red
  As the stained stones kissed by the English dead.
Kindness of wooed and wooer
Seems shame to their love pure.
O Love, your eyes lose lure
  When I behold eyes blinded in my stead!

Your slender attitude
  Trembles not exquisite like limbs knife-skewed,
Rolling and rolling there
Where God seems not to care;
Till the fierce love they bear
  Cramps them in death's extreme decrepitude.

Your voice sings not so soft,—
  Though even as wind murmuring through raftered loft,—
Your dear voice is not dear,
Gentle, and evening clear,
As theirs whom none now hear,
  Now earth has stopped their piteous mouths that coughed.

Heart, you were never hot
  Nor large, nor full like hearts made great with shot;
And though your hand be pale,
Paler are all which trail
Your cross through flame and hail:
  Weep, you may weep, for you may touch them not.

BM has five drafts, two of them cancelled. The text given here
follows a fair copy, with last-moment changes, made by Owen, and
presented to E. Blunden by S. Sassoon.
l. 4: BM (a) has *seems weak* (not cancelled), and *shame* in the margin.
l. 8: all BM drafts have *beautiful*: *exquisite* is given by EB.
l. 10: earlier drafts give *Where God seems not to care*; BM (a)
substitutes *skies* for *God*
l. 18: BM (a) has *gagged*

The Parable of the Old Man and the Young

So Abram rose, and clave the wood, and went,
And took the fire with him, and a knife.
And as they sojourned both of them together,
Isaac the first-born spake and said, My Father,
Behold the preparations, fire and iron,
But where the lamb for this burnt-offering?
Then Abram bound the youth with belts and straps,
And builded parapets and trenches there,
And stretchèd forth the knife to slay his son.
When lo! an angel called him out of heaven,
Saying, Lay not thy hand upon the lad,
Neither do anything to him. Behold,
A ram, caught in a thicket by its horns;
Offer the Ram of Pride instead of him.
But the old man would not so, but slew his son,
And half the seed of Europe, one by one.

BM has one draft. OS has one draft.
EB and SS give *MEN* in title: BM gives *MAN*.
l. 8: BM has *And built a parapet of earth and wood*, deleted.
ll. 12–16: OS gives

> *Neither do anything to him, thy son.*
> *Behold! Caught in a thicket by its horns*
> *A Ram. Offer the Ram of Pride instead.*
> *But the old man would not so, but slew his son.*

l. 16: omitted by SS.

Arms and the Boy

Let the boy try along this bayonet-blade
How cold steel is, and keen with hunger of blood;
Blue with all malice, like a madman's flash;
And thinly drawn with famishing for flesh.

Lend him to stroke these blind, blunt bullet-leads
Which long to nuzzle in the hearts of lads,
Or give him cartridges of fine zinc teeth,
Sharp with the sharpness of grief and death.

For his teeth seem for laughing round an apple.
There lurk no claws behind his fingers supple;
And God will grow no talons at his heels,
Nor antlers through the thickness of his curls.

BM has two drafts. OS has one draft, dated *3.5.18*.
l. *5*: EB gives *bullet-heads*

Anthem for Doomed Youth

What passing-bells for these who die as cattle?
　Only the monstrous anger of the guns.
　Only the stuttering rifles' rapid rattle
Can patter out their hasty orisons.
No mockeries now for them; no prayers nor bells,
　Nor any voice of mourning save the choirs,—
The shrill, demented choirs of wailing shells;
　And bugles calling for them from sad shires.

What candles may be held to speed them all?
　Not in the hands of boys, but in their eyes
Shall shine the holy glimmers of good-byes.
　The pallor of girls' brows shall be their pall;
Their flowers the tenderness of patient minds,
And each slow dusk a drawing-down of blinds.

BM has four drafts. HO has two, together with a draft of the first six lines. LG has one draft.

The poem is entitled *Anthem for Dead Youth* in the earlier drafts: in the final one, *Dead* is cancelled and *Doomed* substituted.

l. 5: EB gives *No mockeries for them from prayers or bells*. The line appears thus in the final draft, but with *from* and *or* cancelled, and *no* and *nor* written above; also, *now* is inserted below *mockeries*.

l. 13: BM (a) has alternatives, *silent* and *patient*, together with a deleted variant, *sweet white*. The previous drafts show a large number of variants for the epithet. Owen did not hit upon *silent* till the final draft: *patient* was then pencilled in, presumably at SS's suggestion when Owen showed him the poem at Craiglockhart in September, 1917.

Silent contrasts with the various loud noises featured in the octave, and chimes with the plangent long *i*'s of the sestet—Owen's *sweet white* suggests that he needed this sound here. But *patient* gives the stronger sense, and carries on the alliteration of the previous line and the first five lines of the octave.

An early BM draft, substituting *you* for *these*, makes the poem more
directly personal—

Anthem for Dead Youth

What passing-bells for you who die in herds?
   —Only the monstrous anger of the guns!
   —Only the stuttering rifles' rattled words
Can patter out your hasty orisons.
No chants for you, nor balms, nor wreaths, nor bells,
   Nor any voice of mourning, save the choirs,
⎰And long-drawn sighs of wailing shells;
⎱~~The shrill demented choirs~~
   And bugles calling for you from sad shires.

What candles may we hold to speed you all?
   Not in the hands of boys, but in their eyes
Shall shine [the] holy lights of our goodbyes.
   The pallor of girls' brows must be your pall.
Your flowers, the tenderness of comrades' minds,
And each slow dusk, a drawing-down of blinds.

The Send-Off

Down the close, darkening lanes they sang their way
To the siding-shed,
And lined the train with faces grimly gay.

Their breasts were stuck all white with wreath and spray
As men's are, dead.

Dull porters watched them, and a casual tramp
Stood staring hard,
Sorry to miss them from the upland camp.
Then, unmoved, signals nodded, and a lamp
Winked to the guard.

So secretly, like wrongs hushed-up, they went.
They were not ours:
We never heard to which front these were sent.

Nor there if they yet mock what women meant
Who gave them flowers.

Shall they return to beatings of great bells
In wild train-loads?
A few, a few, too few for drums and yells,
May creep back, silent, to still village wells
Up half-known roads.

BM has five drafts, three entitled *The Draft*. HO has one part-draft.
Owen evidently had difficulty in deciding the form of this poem:
the earlier drafts begin, respectively—

 (i) *Softly down darkening lanes they sang their way*
 And no word said.
 They filled the train with faces vaguely gay
 And shoulders covered all white with wreath and spray
 As men's are, dead.

(ii) *Low-voiced through darkening lanes they sang their way to the cattle-shed.*
   And filled the train with faces grimly gay.
   Their breasts were stuck all white with wreath and spray, as men's are, dead.

(iii) *Down the wet darkening lanes they sang their way to the cattle-shed*
   And lined the train with faces grimly gay.
   Their breasts were stuck all white with wreath and spray
   As men's are, dead.

1. 19: all five drafts have *to still village wells*. In the final draft, however, followed by EB, *still* is cancelled, as is an alternative, *strange*. Both metre and rhythm require a monosyllable here, and it seems probable that Owen would have inserted one in a final revision. I have therefore restored *still*.

The part-draft appears in a letter home, dated May 4, 1918, in which Owen writes, *I have long 'waited' for a final stanza to* The Draft (*which begins*—

1

"Down the deep, darkening lanes they sang their way
To the waiting train,
And filled its doors with faces grimly gay,
And heads and shoulders white with wreath and spray,
As men's are, slain."

*   *   *

4

Will they return, to beatings of great bells,
In wild train-loads?
A few, a few, too few for drums and yells,
May walk back, silent, to their village wells,
Up half-known roads.

Exposure

Our brains ache, in the merciless iced east winds that knive
    us . . .
Wearied we keep awake because the night is silent . . .
Low, drooping flares confuse our memory of the salient . . .
Worried by silence, sentries whisper, curious, nervous,
        But nothing happens.

Watching, we hear the mad gusts tugging on the wire,
Like twitching agonies of men among its brambles.
Northward, incessantly, the flickering gunnery rumbles,
Far off, like a dull rumour of some other war.
        What are we doing here?

The poignant misery of dawn begins to grow . . .
We only know war lasts, rain soaks, and clouds sag stormy.
Dawn massing in the east her melancholy army
Attacks once more in ranks on shivering ranks of gray,
        But nothing happens.

Sudden successive flights of bullets streak the silence.
Less deathly than the air that shudders black with snow,
With sidelong flowing flakes that flock, pause, and renew;
We watch them wandering up and down the wind's non-
    chalance,
        But nothing happens.

Pale flakes with fingering stealth come feeling for our faces—
We cringe in holes, back on forgotten dreams, and stare,
    snow-dazed,
Deep into grassier ditches. So we drowse, sun-dozed,
Littered with blossoms trickling where the blackbird fusses.
        Is it that we are dying?

Slowly our ghosts drag home: glimpsing the sunk fires,
    glozed
With crusted dark-red jewels; crickets jingle there;
For hours the innocent mice rejoice: the house is theirs;

Shutters and doors, all closed: on us the doors are closed,—
    We turn back to our dying.

Since we believe not otherwise can kind fires burn;
Nor ever suns smile true on child, or field, or fruit.
For God's invincible spring our love is made afraid;
Therefore, not loath, we lie out here; therefore were born,
    For love of God seems dying.

To-night, His frost will fasten on this mud and us,
Shrivelling many hands, puckering foreheads crisp.
The burying-party, picks and shovels in their shaking grasp,
Pause over half-known faces. All their eyes are ice,
    But nothing happens.

BM has two drafts and several part-drafts. Owen dated this poem,
February 1916: EB points out that this must be a slip of the pen
for *February 1917*.
l. 17: EB gives *deadly*
ll. 38–9: *The burying-party, picks and shovels in shaking grasp,*
    ⎰*Look dumbly on their faces,—bricks; their stark eyes,—ice*
    ⎱*Pause over half-known faces; all their eyes are red.*
I am indebted to Dr. Welland for the following notes on the last
six lines of this poem.

> "*Tonight, this frost will fasten on this mud and us,*
> *Shrivelling many hands, puckering foreheads crisp.*

This is a pencilled correction (above the line) of a previously
inserted *the*. I am sure that it is *this*, but there is just enough
ambiguity about it to justify retaining EB's preferable reading.
Similarly, the pencilled correction to the last line of the previous
stanza appears to have *the* inserted between *for* and *love*, but the
horizontal line may be read either as the crossing of the *t* or as a
cancellation.
l. 39: It is possible to read the last word as *red* because of an ink
loop above the final letter, but it is surely a slip of the pen: the
half-rhyme demands *ice* which he uses in two previous attempts at
this line (once on each sheet)."

The Show

We have fallen in the dreams the ever-living
Breathe on the tarnished mirror of the world,
And then smooth out with ivory hands and sigh.
W. B. YEATS

My soul looked down from a vague height, with Death,
As unremembering how I rose or why,
And saw a sad land, weak with sweats of dearth,
Gray, cratered like the moon with hollow woe,
And pitted with great pocks and scabs of plagues.

Across its beard, that horror of harsh wire,
There moved thin caterpillars, slowly uncoiled.
It seemed they pushed themselves to be as plugs
Of ditches, where they writhed and shrivelled, killed.

By them had slimy paths been trailed and scraped
Round myriad warts that might be little hills.

From gloom's last dregs these long-strung creatures crept,
And vanished out of dawn down hidden holes.

(And smell came up from those foul openings
As out of mouths, or deep wounds deepening.)

On dithering feet upgathered, more and more,
Brown strings, towards strings of gray, with bristling spines,
All migrants from green fields, intent on mire.

Those that were gray, of more abundant spawns,
Ramped on the rest and ate them and were eaten.

I saw their bitten backs curve, loop, and straighten,
I watched those agonies curl, lift, and flatten.
Whereat, in terror what that sight might mean,
I reeled and shivered earthward like a feather.

And Death fell with me, like a deepening moan.

And He, picking a manner of worm, which half had hid
Its bruises in the earth, but crawled no further,
Showed me its feet, the feet of many men,
And the fresh-severed head of it, my head.

BM has one draft: HO has one early draft, heavily corrected and
untitled.
ll. 1–5: HO, *He looked down, from the great height of death,*
　　　　　　Having forgotten how he died, and why.
　　　　　　He saw the earth face grey and sunk with dearth
　　　　　　And cratered like the moon's with hollow woe,
　　　　　　All pitted with great pocks and scabs of plague.
l. 6: BM has, Across ⌠*the horror of its beard of wire,* deleted.
　　　　　　　　　　 ⌡*its horrid beard of prickly wire,*
In a letter to his mother, dated January 19, 1917, Owen writes that
No Man's Land *is pockmarked like a body of foulest disease and its
odour is the breath of cancer . . . No Man's Land under snow is
like the face of the moon, chaotic, crater-ridden, uninhabitable, awful,
the abode of madness.*

Spring Offensive

Halted against the shade of a last hill,
They fed, and lying easy, were at ease
And, finding comfortable chests and knees,
Carelessly slept. But many there stood still
To face the stark, blank sky beyond the ridge,
Knowing their feet had come to the end of the world.

Marvelling they stood, and watched the long grass swirled
By the May breeze, murmurous with wasp and midge,
For though the summer oozed into their veins
Like an injected drug for their bodies' pains,
Sharp on their souls hung the imminent line of grass,
Fearfully flashed the sky's mysterious glass.

Hour after hour they ponder the warm field—
And the far valley behind, where the buttercup
Had blessed with gold their slow boots coming up,
Where even the little brambles would not yield,
But clutched and clung to them like sorrowing hands;
They breathe like trees unstirred.

Till like a cold gust thrills the little word
At which each body and its soul begird
And tighten them for battle. No alarms
Of bugles, no high flags, no clamorous haste—
Only a lift and flare of eyes that faced
The sun, like a friend with whom their love is done.
O larger shone that smile against the sun,—
Mightier than his whose bounty these have spurned.

So, soon they topped the hill, and raced together
Over an open stretch of herb and heather
Exposed. And instantly the whole sky burned
With fury against them; earth set sudden cups
In thousands for their blood; and the green slope
Chasmed and steepened sheer to infinite space.

*   *   *

Of them who running on that last high place
Leapt to swift unseen bullets, or went up
On the hot blast and fury of hell's upsurge,
Or plunged and fell away past this world's verge,
Some say God caught them even before they fell.

But what say such as from existence' brink
Ventured but drave too swift to sink,
The few who rushed in the body to enter hell,
And there out-fiending all its fiends and flames
With superhuman inhumanities,
Long-famous glories, immemorial shames—
And crawling slowly back, have by degrees
Regained cool peaceful air in wonder—
Why speak not they of comrades that went under?

BM has one draft: SS has one part-draft, ending *But clutched and clung to them like sorrowing arms*, and with a footnote by Owen, *Is this worth going on with? | I don't want to write anything to which a soldier would say No Compris!*
l. 10: SS. *Like the injected drug for their bones' pains,*
l. 14: SS. *buttercups*
l. 18: BM has *All their strange day* cancelled at the beginning of this line. The words weaken the line: on the other hand, Owen would probably have written a substitute for them in a final revision, since the other short lines in BM (39, 45) also have indications of being unfinished.
ll. 30–1: SS. *and soft sudden cups Opened in thousands for their blood:* this version, deleted, appears in BM.
l. 31: SS. *slopes*
l. 34: I follow EB's reading, though it is cancelled in the BM MS. I am indebted to Dr. Welland for the following note on this line—
"My impression is that Owen changed it as follows:
(a) *unseen* was cancelled and *surf of* substituted above
(b) he then cancelled *Leapt to the unseen* and substituted above *Breasted the shrieking*
(c) next he cancelled *the shrieking*, put in another *the* before it and *even rapture of bullets* after it, and then cancelled *Breasted*
The best alternative to EB I can suggest is

Breasted the surf of bullets, or went up

I can find no MS. authority for EB's *swift unseen bullets*; what I read as *surf of* he reads as *swift*, but then its placing suggests it ought to come after *unseen*. The only virtue of my emendation is that it retains the swimming image that WO's changes indicate he was developing here; *surf of* has been underlined but not cancelled, and I can see no way of satisfactorily using the *even rapture of bullets*.

l. 39: BM shows a gap between *Ventured* and *but*, suggesting that Owen would, in a final revision, have inserted a word to lengthen this line to the normal five-stress metre of the poem.

l. 45: BM gives *the cool & peaceful air*, with *the* cancelled. EB has, I believe, mistaken the ampersand for a comma, but the sign is similar to an ampersand between *fiends* and *flames* four lines above. Here again I think Owen would have made a five-stress line in final revision."

Dulce Et Decorum Est

Bent double, like old beggars under sacks,
Knock-kneed, coughing like hags, we cursed through sludge,
Till on the haunting flares we turned our backs
And towards our distant rest began to trudge.
Men marched asleep. Many had lost their boots
But limped on, blood-shod. All went lame; all blind;
Drunk with fatigue; deaf even to the hoots
Of tired, outstripped Five-Nines that dropped behind.

Gas! GAS! Quick, boys!—An ecstasy of fumbling,
Fitting the clumsy helmets just in time;
But someone still was yelling out and stumbling
And flound'ring like a man in fire or lime . . .
Dim, through the misty panes and thick green light,
As under a green sea, I saw him drowning.

In all my dreams, before my helpless sight,
He plunges at me, guttering, choking, drowning.

If in some smothering dreams you too could pace
Behind the wagon that we flung him in,
And watch the white eyes writhing in his face,
His hanging face, like a devil's sick of sin;
If you could hear, at every jolt, the blood
Come gargling from the froth-corrupted lungs,
Obscene as cancer, bitter as the cud
Of vile, incurable sores on innocent tongues,—
My friend, you would not tell with such high zest
To children ardent for some desperate glory,
The old Lie: Dulce et decorum est
Pro patria mori.

BM has two drafts, the earlier of which gives, beneath the title,
To Jessie Pope etc (cancelled), and *To a certain Poetess*. HO has two
drafts, one subscribed *To Jessie Pope etc*, the other, *To a certain
Poetess*.

In a letter to his mother, dated August 1917, Owen wrote *Here is a gas poem, done yesterday.*

l. 8: BM (a) has *tired, outstripped* $\begin{cases} gas\text{-}shells \\ Five\text{-}Nines \end{cases}$ deleted, and the line reads *Of gas-shells dropping softly that dropped behind.* EB amended to *Of gas-shells dropping softly behind.* The earlier BM draft shows two alternatives for this line, both of ten syllables. HO (a) gives *Of tired, outstripped five-nines that dropped behind.* HO (b) gives *Of disappointed shells that dropped behind.*
After line 8, BM (b) has four lines which in the later version were first altered a little, then cancelled—

> *Then somewhere near in front: Whew . . . fup . . . fop . . . fup . . .*
> *Gas-shells or duds? We loosened masks, in case—*
> *And listened . . . Nothing . . . Far rumouring of Krupp . . .*
> *Then stinging poison hit us in the face.*

l. 20: HO (b) *His hanging face, tortured for your own sin*
l. 23: EB omits *Obscene as cancer*
ll. 23–4: these were substituted, at a late stage of composition, for
> *And think how, once, his head was like a bud,*
> *Fresh as a country rose, and keen, and young,—*

Asleep

Under his helmet, up against his pack,
After the many days of work and waking,
Sleep took him by the brow and laid him back.
And in the happy no-time of his sleeping,
Death took him by the heart. There was a quaking
Of the aborted life within him leaping . . .
Then chest and sleepy arms once more fell slack.
And soon the slow, stray blood came creeping
From the intrusive lead, like ants on track.

    *   *   *

Whether his deeper sleep lie shaded by the shaking
Of great wings, and the thoughts that hung the stars,
High pillowed on calm pillows of God's making
Above these clouds, these rains, these sleets of lead,
And these winds' scimitars;
—Or whether yet his thin and sodden head
Confuses more and more with the low mould,
His hair being one with the grey grass
And finished fields of autumns that are old . . .
Who knows? Who hopes? Who troubles? Let it pass!
He sleeps. He sleeps less tremulous, less cold
Than we who must awake, and waking, say Alas!

BM has three drafts, one entitled *Lines on a soldier whom shrapnel killed asleep*. LG has one draft, dated *Nov. 14, 1917*.
         the aborted life
l. 6: BM (b), *Of frustrated ~~life like child~~ within him leaping,*
l. 9: BM (b), *From under that collapse like ants on track.*
l. 12: BM (a), *And pillowed on high pillows of God's making,*
l. 18: LG, *Of finished fields, and wire-scrags rusty-old,*
In a letter to LG, with whom he had just spent a day's leave, enclosing the above poem, Owen describes how, walking back to Winchester alone *over the long backs of the downs*, he *could almost see the dead lying about in the hollows of the downs.*

Futility

Move him into the sun—
Gently its touch awoke him once,
At home, whispering of fields unsown.
Always it woke him, even in France,
Until this morning and this snow.
If anything might rouse him now
The kind old sun will know.

Think how it wakes the seeds,—
Woke, once, the clays of a cold star.
Are limbs, so dear-achieved, are sides,
Full-nerved—still warm—too hard to stir?
Was it for this the clay grew tall?
—O what made fatuous sunbeams toil
To break earth's sleep at all?

BM has two drafts, one of them cancelled. Dr. D. S. R. Welland
possesses facsimiles of two drafts, which were owned by the late
Miss Vera Hewland, and are believed to have been destroyed
after her death in 1960. In both, l. 3 is *In Wales, whispering of
fields unsown.*
ll. 10–11: BM (a) has

> *Are limbs,* { *so dear achieved, are*
> *perfect at last, and sides*
>
> { *Full*
> { *Warm—nerved,—still warm,—too hard to stir?*
> { *Rich*

BM (b) has two variants—

> *bled*
> *Are limbs, pricked with a little sword,*
> *Yet limbs—still warm—too hard to stir?*
>
> *Are limbs, so ready for life, full-grown,*
> *Nerved and still·warm—too hard to stir?*

The Last Laugh

'O Jesus Christ! I'm hit,' he said; and died.
Whether he vainly cursed, or prayed indeed,
The Bullets chirped—In vain! vain! vain!
Machine-guns chuckled,—Tut-tut! Tut-tut!
And the Big Gun guffawed.

Another sighed,—'O Mother, mother! Dad!'
Then smiled, at nothing, childlike, being dead.
    And the lofty Shrapnel-cloud
    Leisurely gestured,—Fool!
    And the falling splinters tittered.

'My Love!' one moaned. Love-languid seemed his mood,
Till, slowly lowered, his whole face kissed the mud.
    And the Bayonets' long teeth grinned;
    Rabbles of Shells hooted and groaned;
    And the Gas hissed.

HO has one draft. OS has two drafts, one entitled *The Last Word*.
l. 10: OS, *And the Splinters spat and tittered.*
An earlier draft, entitled *Last Words*, was enclosed in a letter to
his mother, dated February 18, 1918:

> *"O Jesus Christ!" one fellow sighed.*
> *And kneeled, and bowed, tho' not in prayer, and died.*
>   *And the Bullets sang "In Vain",*
>   *Machine Guns chuckled "Vain",*
>   *Big Guns guffawed "In Vain".*
>
> *"Father and mother!" one boy said.*
> *Then smiled—at nothing, like a small child; being dead.*
>   *And the Shrapnel Cloud*
>   *Slowly gestured "Vain",*
>   *The falling splinters muttered "Vain".*
>
> *"My love!" another cried, "My love, my bud!"*
> *Then, gently lowered, his whole face kissed the mud.*
>   *And the Flares gesticulated, "Vain",*
>   *The Shells hooted, "In Vain",*
>   *And the Gas hissed, "In Vain."*

The Letter

With B.E.F. June 10. Dear Wife,
(O blast this pencil. 'Ere, Bill, lend's a knife.)
I'm in the pink at present, dear.
I think the war will end this year.
We don't see much of them square-'eaded 'Uns.
We're out of harm's way, not bad fed.
I'm longing for a taste of your old buns.
(Say, Jimmie, spare's a bite of bread.)
There don't seem much to say just now.
(Yer what? Then don't, yer ruddy cow!
And give us back me cigarette!)
I'll soon be 'ome. You mustn't fret.
My feet's improvin', as I told you of.
We're out in rest now. Never fear.
(VRACH! By crumbs, but that was near.)
Mother might spare you half a sov.
Kiss Nell and Bert. When me and you—
(Eh? What the 'ell! Stand to? Stand to!
Jim, give's a hand with pack on, lad.
Guh! Christ! I'm hit. Take 'old. Aye, bad.
No, damn your iodine. Jim? 'Ere!
Write my old girl, Jim, there's a dear.)

BM has one draft.

The Sentry

We'd found an old Boche dug-out, and he knew,
And gave us hell, for shell on frantic shell
Hammered on top, but never quite burst through.
Rain, guttering down in waterfalls of slime,
Kept slush waist-high and rising hour by hour,
And choked the steps too thick with clay to climb.
What murk of air remained stank old, and sour
With fumes of whizz-bangs, and the smell of men
Who'd lived there years, and left their curse in the den,
If not their corpses. . . .
                              There we herded from the blast
Of whizz-bangs, but one found our door at last,—
Buffeting eyes and breath, snuffing the candles,
And thud! flump! thud! down the steep steps came thumping
And sploshing in the flood, deluging muck—
The sentry's body; then, his rifle, handles
Of old Boche bombs, and mud in ruck on ruck.
We dredged him up, for killed, until he whined
"O sir, my eyes—I'm blind—I'm blind, I'm blind!"
Coaxing, I held a flame against his lids
And said if he could see the least blurred light
He was not blind; in time he'd get all right.
"I can't," he sobbed. Eyeballs, huge-bulged like squids',
Watch my dreams still; but I forgot him there
In posting Next for duty, and sending a scout
To beg a stretcher somewhere, and flound'ring about
To other posts under the shrieking air.

*   *   *

Those other wretches, how they bled and spewed,
And one who would have drowned himself for good,—
I try not to remember these things now.
Let dread hark back for one word only: how
Half listening to that sentry's moans and jumps,
And the wild chattering of his broken teeth,
Renewed most horribly whenever crumps

Pummelled the roof and slogged the air beneath—
Through the dense din, I say, we heard him shout
"I see your lights!" But ours had long died out.

BM has one full draft and a fragment of an earlier draft: SS has
one draft.
ll. 5–6: SS and EB, *Kept slush waist-high that, rising hour by hour,*
Choked up the steps. . . .
In a letter to his mother, dated January 16, 1917, Owen mentions
the episode of a sentry blown down into a dug-out and blinded.

Conscious

His fingers wake, and flutter; up the bed.
His eyes come open with a pull of will,
Helped by the yellow may-flowers by his head.
The blind-cord drawls across the window-sill . . .
What a smooth floor the ward has! What a rug!
Who is that talking somewhere out of sight?
Why are they laughing? What's inside that jug?
"Nurse! Doctor!"—"Yes; all right, all right."

But sudden evening muddles all the air—
There seems no time to want a drink of water,
Nurse looks so far away. And here and there
Music and roses burst through crimson slaughter.
He can't remember where he saw blue sky.
More blankets. Cold. He's cold. And yet so hot.
And there's no light to see the voices by;
There is no time to ask—he knows not what.

BM has three drafts, one in four-line stanzas: EB conflated these:
I follow his text, but for ll. 11 and 12.
ll. 1–4: BM (b) gives

> *His fingers flutter, conscious of the sheet.*
> *His eyes come open with a pull of will,*
> *Helped by the yellow mayflowers on the sill.*
> *—How calm the place is! God! How clean! How sweet!*

l. 7: BM (b), *Three flies are creeping round the shiny jug* . . .
l. 9: BM (b), *But sudden dusk bewilders all the air.*
l. 11: SS and EB give *everywhere*: all BM drafts give *here and there*
l. 12: SS and EB give *burnt*: all BM drafts give *burst*
In a letter dated *May 8, 1917*, written from hospital to his sister
Mary, Owen mentioned *great blue bowls of yellow Mayflowers* in
the ward.

A Terre

(being the philosophy of many soldiers)

Sit on the bed. I'm blind, and three parts shell.
Be careful; can't shake hands now; never shall.
Both arms have mutinied against me,—brutes.
My fingers fidget like ten idle brats.

I tried to peg out soldierly,—no use!
One dies of war like any old disease.
This bandage feels like pennies on my eyes.
I have my medals?—Discs to make eyes close.
My glorious ribbons?—Ripped from my own back
In scarlet shreds. (That's for your poetry book.)

A short life and a merry one, my buck!
We used to say we'd hate to live dead-old,—
Yet now . . . I'd willingly be puffy, bald,
And patriotic. Buffers catch from boys
At least the jokes hurled at them. I suppose
Little I'd ever teach a son, but hitting,
Shooting, war, hunting, all the arts of hurting.
Well, that's what I learnt,—that, and making money.

Your fifty years ahead seem none too many?
Tell me how long I've got? God! For one year
To help myself to nothing more than air!
One Spring! Is one too good to spare, too long?
Spring wind would work its own way to my lung,
And grow me legs as quick as lilac-shoots.

My servant's lamed, but listen how he shouts!
When I'm lugged out, he'll still be good for that.
Here in this mummy-case, you know, I've thought
How well I might have swept his floors for ever.
I'd ask no nights off when the bustle's over,
Enjoying so the dirt. Who's prejudiced
Against a grimed hand when his own's quite dust,
Less live than specks that in the sun-shafts turn,

Less warm than dust that mixes with arms' tan?
I'd love to be a sweep, now, black as Town,
Yes, or a muckman. Must I be his load?

O Life, Life, let me breathe,—a dug-out rat!
Not worse than ours the existences rats lead—
Nosing along at night down some safe rut,
They find a shell-proof home before they rot.
Dead men may envy living mites in cheese,
Or good germs even. Microbes have their joys,
And subdivide, and never come to death.
Certainly flowers have the easiest time on earth.
"I shall be one with nature, herb, and stone",
Shelley would tell me. Shelley would be stunned:
The dullest Tommy hugs that fancy now.
"Pushing up daisies" is their creed, you know.
To grain, then, go my fat, to buds my sap,
For all the usefulness there is in soap.
D'you think the Boche will ever stew man-soup?
Some day, no doubt, if . . .

                              Friend, be very sure
I shall be better off with plants that share
More peaceably the meadow and the shower.
Soft rains will touch me,—as they could touch once,
And nothing but the sun shall make me ware.
Your guns may crash around me. I'll not hear;
Or, if I wince, I shall not know I wince.
Don't take my soul's poor comfort for your jest.
Soldiers may grow a soul when turned to fronds,
But here the thing's best left at home with friends.

My soul's a little grief, grappling your chest,
To climb your throat on sobs; easily chased
On other sighs and wiped by fresher winds.

Carry my crying spirit till it's weaned
To do without what blood remained these wounds.

BM has one draft. For an interesting earlier draft of this poem, see Appendix 3.

l. 11: SS, *my brick*

l. 37: BM originally had *Not worse than fighting-men's the life rats led*. Owen altered to the text here printed, except that he later substituted *lives* for *existences*: I have followed SS and EB in restoring *existences*.

l. 38: SS, *some safe vat*—a misreading of Owen's handwriting.

In a letter to his mother, dated April 1918, Owen wrote *This afternoon I was retouching a photographic representation of an officer dying of wounds*, and quotes a version of the first twelve lines of the poem above.

Disabled

He sat in a wheeled chair, waiting for dark,
And shivered in his ghastly suit of grey,
Legless, sewn short at elbow. Through the park
Voices of boys rang saddening like a hymn,
Voices of play and pleasure after day,
Till gathering sleep had mothered them from him.

    *   *   *

About this time Town used to swing so gay
When glow-lamps budded in the light blue trees,
And girls glanced lovelier as the air grew dim,—
In the old times, before he threw away his knees.
Now he will never feel again how slim
Girls' waists are, or how warm their subtle hands;
All of them touch him like some queer disease.

    *   *   *

There was an artist silly for his face,
For it was younger than his youth, last year.
Now, he is old; his back will never brace;
He's lost his colour very far from here,
Poured it down shell-holes till the veins ran dry,
And half his lifetime lapsed in the hot race,
And leap of purple spurted from his thigh.

    *   *   *

One time he liked a blood-smear down his leg,
After the matches, carried shoulder-high.
It was after football, when he'd drunk a peg,
He thought he'd better join.—He wonders why.
Someone had said he'd look a god in kilts,
That's why; and may be, too, to please his Meg;
Aye, that was it, to please the giddy jilts
He asked to join. He didn't have to beg;
Smiling they wrote his lie; aged nineteen years.
Germans he scarcely thought of; all their guilt,
And Austria's, did not move him. And no fears
Of Fear came yet. He thought of jewelled hilts
For daggers in plaid socks; of smart salutes;
And care of arms; and leave; and pay arrears;

Esprit de corps; and hints for young recruits.
And soon, he was drafted out with drums and cheers.

*   *   *

Some cheered him home, but not as crowds cheer Goal.
Only a solemn man who brought him fruits
Thanked him; and then inquired about his soul.

*   *   *

Now, he will spend a few sick years in Institutes,
And do what things the rules consider wise,
And take whatever pity they may dole.
To-night he noticed how the women's eyes
Passed from him to the strong men that were whole.
How cold and late it is! Why don't they come
And put him into bed? Why don't they come?

BM has two drafts, and a fragment. OS has one draft. The earlier
BM gives a stanza, later cancelled, between the present stanzas
two and three—

> *Ah! He was handsome when he used to stand*
> *Each evening on the curb or by the quays.*
> *His old soft cap slung half-way down his ear;*
> *Proud of his neck, scarfed with a sunburn band,*
> *And of his curl, and all his reckless gear,*
> *Down to the gloves of sun-brown on his hand.*

In a letter to his mother, dated October 14, 1917, Owen said that
SS when they were together showed him [Robert Graves] *my longish
war-piece*, Disabled.

Mental Cases

Who are these? Why sit they here in twilight?
Wherefore rock they, purgatorial shadows,
Drooping tongues from jaws that slob their relish,
Baring teeth that leer like skulls' teeth wicked?
Stroke on stroke of pain,—but what slow panic,
Gouged these chasms round their fretted sockets?
Ever from their hair and through their hands' palms
Misery swelters. Surely we have perished
Sleeping, and walk hell; but who these hellish?

—These are men whose minds the Dead have ravished.
Memory fingers in their hair of murders,
Multitudinous murders they once witnessed.
Wading sloughs of flesh these helpless wander,
Treading blood from lungs that had loved laughter.
Always they must see these things and hear them,
Batter of guns and shatter of flying muscles,
Carnage incomparable, and human squander
Rucked too thick for these men's extrication.

Therefore still their eyeballs shrink tormented
Back into their brains, because on their sense
Sunlight seems a blood-smear; night comes blood-black;
Dawn breaks open like a wound that bleeds afresh.
—Thus their heads wear this hilarious, hideous,
Awful falseness of set-smiling corpses.
—Thus their hands are plucking at each other;
Picking at the rope-knouts of their scourging;
Snatching after us who smote them, brother,
Pawing us who dealt them war and madness.

BM has one finished draft, with alternative title, *The Aliens*, deleted. BM has also a fragmentary draft, possibly an early attempt at this poem, with cancelled title, *Purgatorial Passions*. OS has one draft. Dr. Welland possesses a facsimile of a draft, entitled *The Deranged*, formerly owned by Miss Vera Hewland, and believed to have been destroyed after her death in 1960.

After the last line BM (a) has a space, then *Time will not make*: since these four words are not cancelled, we may presume that Owen had an idea of continuing the poem.

In a letter to his mother, dated May 26, 1918, Owen wrote *I've been busy this evening with my terrific poem (at present) called* The Deranged.

l. 19: OS, *twinge tormented*

l. 22: OS, *wound fresh-bleeding.*

ll. 25–28: OS, *Thus their fingers pick and pluck each other,—*
Picking the hard scourge that scourged them, brother,
Plucking us who dealt them war and madness.

The Chances

I mind as 'ow the night afore that show
Us five got talkin',—we was in the know.
"Over the top to-morrer; boys, we're for it.
First wave we are, first ruddy wave; that's tore it!"
"Ah well," says Jimmy,—an' 'e's seen some scrappin'—
"There ain't no more nor five things as can 'appen:
Ye get knocked out; else wounded—bad or cushy;
Scuppered; or nowt except yer feelin' mushy."

One of us got the knock-out, blown to chops.
T'other was 'urt, like, losin' both 'is props.
An' one, to use the word of 'ypocrites,
'Ad the misfortoon to be took be Fritz.
Now me, I wasn't scratched, praise God Amighty,
(Though next time please I'll thank 'im for a blighty).
But poor young Jim, 'e's livin' an' 'e's not;
'E reckoned 'e'd five chances, an' 'e 'ad;
'E's wounded, killed, and pris'ner, all the lot,
The bloody lot all rolled in one. Jim's mad.

BM has three drafts: HO has two drafts. The spelling in the text
above follows BM, which EB amended.
l. 6: EB omits *no*.
l. 10: BM has *loosin'*

The Dead-Beat

He dropped,—more sullenly than wearily,
Lay stupid like a cod, heavy like meat,
And none of us could kick him to his feet;
Just blinked at my revolver, blearily;
—Didn't appear to know a war was on,
Or see the blasted trench at which he stared.
"I'll do 'em in," he whined. "If this hand's spared,
I'll murder them, I will."

                    A low voice said,
"It's Blighty, p'raps, he sees; his pluck's all gone,
Dreaming of all the valiant, that aren't dead:
Bold uncles, smiling ministerially;
Maybe his brave young wife, getting her fun
In some new home, improved materially.
It's not these stiffs have crazed him; nor the Hun."

We sent him down at last, out of the way.
Unwounded;—stout lad, too, before that strafe.
Malingering? Stretcher-bearers winked, "Not half!"

Next day I heard the Doc.'s well-whiskied laugh:
"That scum you sent last night soon died. Hooray."

BM has one draft. HO has six earlier drafts and part-drafts, two written in four-line stanzas, one dated *Sept. 1917*, another *Oct. 1917.* LG has one draft, in four-line stanzas, with (TRUE, *in the incidental*) written beside the title, which I print below. In a letter to LG, dated *22 Aug. 1917,* enclosing this draft, Owen said, *after leaving him, I wrote something in Sassoon's style.*

> He dropped, more sullenly than wearily,
>   Became a lump of stench, a clot of meat,
>   And none of us could kick him to his feet.
> He blinked at my revolver, blearily.
>
> He didn't seem to know a war was on,
>   Or see or smell the bloody trench at all . . .
>   Perhaps he saw the crowd at Caxton Hall,
> And that is why the fellow's pluck's all gone—

Not that the Kaiser frowns imperially.
  He sees his wife, how cosily she chats;
  Not his blue pal there, feeding fifty rats.
Hotels he sees, improved materially;

Where ministers smile ministerially.
  Sees Punch still grinning at the Belcher bloke;
  Bairnsfather, enlarging on his little joke,
While Belloc prophecies of last year, serially.

We sent him down at last, he seemed so bad,
  Although a strongish chap and quite unhurt.
  Next day I heard the Doc's fat laugh: "That dirt
You sent me down last night's just died. So glad!"

Against ll. 13 and 16, Owen has written *These lines are years old!!*
Against ll. 19–20, *Those are the very words!*

S.I.W.

I will to the King,
And offer him consolation in his trouble,
For that man there has set his teeth to die,
And being one that hates obedience,
Discipline, and orderliness of life,
I cannot mourn him.

W. B. YEATS

I. THE PROLOGUE

Patting good-bye, doubtless they told the lad
He'd always show the Hun a brave man's face;
Father would sooner him dead than in disgrace,—
Was proud to see him going, aye, and glad.
Perhaps his mother whimpered how she'd fret
Until he got a nice safe wound to nurse.
Sisters would wish girls too could shoot, charge, curse;
Brothers—would send his favourite cigarette.
Each week, month after month, they wrote the same,
Thinking him sheltered in some Y.M. Hut,
Because he said so, writing on his butt
Where once an hour a bullet missed its aim
And misses teased the hunger of his brain.
His eyes grew old with wincing, and his hand
Reckless with ague. Courage leaked, as sand
From the best sand-bags after years of rain.
But never leave, wound, fever, trench-foot, shock,
Untrapped the wretch. And death seemed still withheld
For torture of lying machinally shelled,
At the pleasure of this world's Powers who'd run amok.

He'd seen men shoot their hands, on night patrol.
Their people never knew. Yet they were vile.
"Death sooner than dishonour, that's the style!"
So Father said.

II. THE ACTION

One dawn, our wire patrol
Carried him. This time, Death had not missed.

We could do nothing but wipe his bleeding cough.
Could it be accident?—Rifles go off . . .
Not sniped? No. (Later they found the English ball.)

III. THE POEM

It was the reasoned crisis of his soul
Against more days of inescapable thrall,
Against infrangibly wired and blind trench wall
Curtained with fire, roofed in with creeping fire,
Slow grazing fire, that would not burn him whole
But kept him for death's promises and scoff,
And life's half-promising, and both their riling.

IV. THE EPILOGUE

With him they buried the muzzle his teeth had kissed,
And truthfully wrote the Mother, "Tim died smiling".

BM has one draft. HO has an early draft, written in four-line
stanzas. *S.I.W.* is an abbreviation for Self-Inflicted Wound.
l. 4: BM has *aye* with the *e* deleted.
l. 11: SS omits this line.
l. 19: BM has *hourly* and *regularly*, both cancelled, and *machinally*
substituted.
ll. 30–5: heavily corrected in BM: it seems clear that Owen would
have wished to do more work on this section of the poem.
l. 30: BM has *Against the rack that would not kill him whole*, and
Against war, and its no more bearable thrall, both deleted.
l. 31: BM has *infranchibly* [sic], and *dungeoning* cancelled in favour
of *blind*
l. 34: BM has *life's riling and reviling*, deleted; *death's perjury and
{riling—*
{*ruling* deleted but for *death's*; and finally *promises and scoffs*, with
the final s's cancelled.
l. 35: BM has *And* and *For* both cancelled at the beginning of the
line.
SS gives this passage—

> *It was the reasoned crisis of his soul.*
> *Against the fires that would not burn him whole*
> *But kept him for death's perjury and scoff*
> *And life's half-promising, and both their riling.*

A MS. formerly in the possession of the late Miss Vera Hewland, which is believed to have been destroyed after her death, gave the following poem—an early version of *S.I.W.*

HE DIED SMILING

Patting goodbye, his father said, "My lad,
  You'll always show the Hun a brave man's face.
  I'd rather you were dead than in disgrace.
We're proud to see you going, Jim, we're glad."

His mother whimpered, "Jim, my boy, I frets
  Until ye git a nice safe wound, I do."
  His sisters said: why couldn't they go too.
His brothers said they'd send him cigarettes.

For three years, once a week, they wrote the same,
  Adding, "We hope you use the Y.M. Hut."
  And once a day came twenty Navy Cut.
And once an hour a bullet missed its aim.

And misses teased the hunger of his brain.
  His eyes grew scorched with wincing, and his hand
  Reckless with ague. Courage leaked, like sand
From sandbags that have stood three years of rain.

Smile, Smile, Smile

Head to limp head, the sunk-eyed wounded scanned
Yesterday's *Mail*; the casualties (typed small)
And (large) Vast Booty from our Latest Haul.
Also, they read of Cheap Homes, not yet planned
"For," said the paper, "when this war is done
The men's first instinct will be making homes.
Meanwhile their foremost need is aerodromes,
It being certain war has but begun.
Peace would do wrong to our undying dead,--
The sons we offered might regret they died
If we got nothing lasting in their stead.
We must be solidly indemnified.
Though all be worthy Victory which all bought,
We rulers sitting in this ancient spot
Would wrong our very selves if we forgot
The greatest glory will be theirs who fought,
Who kept this nation in integrity."
Nation?—The half-limbed readers did not chafe
But smiled at one another curiously
Like secret men who know their secret safe.
(This is the thing they know and never speak,
That England one by one had fled to France,
Not many elsewhere now, save under France.)
Pictures of these broad smiles appear each week,
And people in whose voice real feeling rings
Say: How they smile! They're happy now, poor things.

23rd September 1918.

BM has one draft: HO has one.
l. 8: SS *just begun.*
l. 18: BM has *lived* deleted in favour of *limbed*
The earlier draft, below, in H.O.'s possession, is written on the
back of a letter to Owen from a brother-officer, dated *11.9.18.* It
is untitled. It is interesting that in this poem—the last, as far as
we know, that Owen wrote—he returned to traditional rhyming.

> *Head to limp head, sunk-eyed wounded scanned*
> *Yesterday's news: the casualties (typed small)*

And (large) *Vast Booty from our Latest Haul.*
Also they read of Cheap Homes, not yet planned,
"For," said the paper, "when the war is done
The men's first instinct will be for their homes.
Meanwhile our need is ships, tanks, aerodromes,
It being certain war is but begun.
Peace would do wrong to our undying dead,
Our glorious sons might even regret they died
If we got nothing lasting in their stead
But lived on, tired and unindemnified.
All will be worthy victory, which all bought.
Yet we who labour on this ancient spot
Would wrong our very selves if we forgot
The greatest glory will be theirs, who fought—
Who kept the nation in integrity."
NATION? *The half-legged, half-lunged did not chafe*
But smiled at one another curiously
Like secret men who know their secret safe.
(This is the thing they know and never speak—
This Nation, one by one, has fled to France
And none lay elsewhere now, save under France.)
Pictures of their broad smiles appear in sketches,
And people say, "They're happy now, poor wretches."

Inspection

"You! What d'you mean by this?" I rapped.
"You dare come on parade like this?"
"Please, sir, it's——" " 'Old yer mouth," the sergeant
    snapped.
"I takes 'is name, sir?"—"Please, and then dismiss."

Some days "confined to camp" he got,
For being "dirty on parade".
He told me, afterwards, the damnèd spot
Was blood, his own. "Well, blood is dirt," I said.

"Blood's dirt," he laughed, looking away
Far off to where his wound had bled
And almost merged for ever into clay.
"The world is washing out its stains," he said.
"It doesn't like our cheeks so red:
Young blood's its great objection.
But when we're duly white-washed, being dead,
The race will bear Field-Marshal God's inspection."

Not in DM. HO has two drafts, the earlier entitled *DIRT*.
l. 10: HO (a) shows *he'd lain and bled* and *his body had bled* rejected
in favour of text above.
l. 15: HO (a), *pipe-clayed* cancelled, and *white-washed* substituted.
HO (b) opens with

> *"Rear rank one pace step back. March!"*
> *I shouted; and inspected the Platoon.*
> *Their necks were craned like collars stiff with starch;*
> *All badges glittered like the great bassoon.*
>
> *Boots dubbined; rifles clean and oiled;*
> *Belts blancoed; straps—The sergeant's cane*
> *Prodded a lad whose haversack was soiled*
> *With some disgraceful muddy stain.*

This version then continues, in four-line stanzas, with the sense of
the HO (a) text.

The Calls

A dismal fog-hoarse siren howls at dawn.
I watch the man it calls for, pushed and drawn
Backwards and forwards, helpless as a pawn.
      But I'm lazy, and his work's crazy.

Quick treble bells begin at nine o'clock,
Scuttling the schoolboy pulling up his sock,
Scaring the late girl in the inky frock.
      I must be crazy; I learn from the daisy.

Stern bells annoy the rooks and doves at ten.
I watch the verger close the doors, and when
I hear the organ moan the first amen,
      Sing my religion's—same as pigeons'.

A blatant bugle tears my afternoons.
Out clump the clumsy Tommies by platoons,
Trying to keep in step with rag-time tunes,
      But I sit still; I've done my drill.

Gongs hum and buzz like saucepan-lids at dusk,
I see a food-hog whet his gold-filled tusk
To eat less bread, and more luxurious rusk.

Then sometimes late at night my window bumps
From gunnery-practice, till my small heart thumps
And listens for the shell-shrieks and the crumps,
      But that's not all.

For leaning out last midnight on my sill
I heard the sighs of men, that have no skill
To speak of their distress, no, nor the will!
      A voice I know. And this time I must go.

BM has one draft. *Calls from my Window* is cancelled and the present
title substituted. The last three stanzas, printed as a separate poem
in EB, seem to me clearly a part of *The Calls*.

After l. 19, BM shows *I've had my fill* and *Here I've no rime that's proper,* both deleted.

l. 23: *And I remember last December*—a reference to Owen's first tour of duty in the trenches—has been cancelled.

l. 27: EB omits *this time.*

At a Calvary near the Ancre

One ever hangs where shelled roads part.
   In this war He too lost a limb,
But His disciples hide apart;
   And now the Soldiers bear with Him.

Near Golgotha strolls many a priest,
   And in their faces there is pride
That they were flesh-marked by the Beast
   By whom the gentle Christ's denied.

The scribes on all the people shove
   And brawl allegiance to the state,
But they who love the greater love
   Lay down their life; they do not hate.

Not in BM. Text taken from a draft in the handwriting of the poet's
mother, in Harold Owen's possession. LG also has a transcript.
l. 10: EB gives *bawl*

Le Christianisme

So the church Christ was hit and buried
　　Under its rubbish and its rubble.
In cellars, packed-up saints lie serried,
　　Well out of hearing of our trouble.

One Virgin still immaculate
　　Smiles on for war to flatter her.
She's halo'd with an old tin hat,
　　But a piece of hell will batter her.

QUIVIÈRES.

Not in BM. HO has one draft.

Soldier's Dream

I dreamed kind Jesus fouled the big-gun gears;
And caused a permanent stoppage in all bolts;
And buckled with a smile Mausers and Colts;
And rusted every bayonet with His tears.

And there were no more bombs, of ours or Theirs,
Not even an old flint-lock, nor even a pikel.
But God was vexed, and gave all power to Michael;
And when I woke he'd seen to our repairs.

The text is taken from a draft sent to O.S. in July or August, 1918·
I give below an earlier version of the poem, of which HO has two
drafts: Owen referred to this version in a letter to SS, dated Novem-
ber 27, 1917, calling it *The last piece from Craiglockhart*: the early
version was therefore written in October, 1917.

> *I dreamed that Christ had fouled the big-gun gears,*
> *And made a permanent stoppage in all bolts*
> *And buckled, with a smile, Mausers and Colts,*
> *And rusted every bayonet with His tears.*
>
> *And there were no more bombs, of ours or Theirs.*
> *So we got out, and gathering up our plunder*
> *Of pains, and nightmares for the night, in wonder!—*
> *Leapt the communication trench like flares.*
>
> *But at the port, a man from U.S.A.*
> *Stopped us, and said: You go right back this minute.*
> *I'll follow. Christ, your miracle ain't in it,*
> *I'll get those rifles mended by today.*

Sonnet

ON SEEING A PIECE OF OUR ARTILLERY
BROUGHT INTO ACTION

Be slowly lifted up, thou long black arm,
Great gun towering towards Heaven, about to curse;
Sway steep against them, and for years rehearse
Huge imprecations like a blasting charm!
Reach at that Arrogance which needs thy harm,
And beat it down before its sins grow worse;
Spend our resentment, cannon,—yea, disburse
Our gold in shapes of flame, our breaths in storm.

Yet, for men's sakes whom thy vast malison
Must wither innocent of enmity,
Be not withdrawn, dark arm, thy spoilure done,
Safe to the bosom of our prosperity.
But when thy spell be cast complete and whole,
May God curse thee, and cut thee from our soul!

BM has one draft.

The Next War

> War's a joke for me and you,
> While we know such dreams are true.
>
> SIEGFRIED SASSOON

Out there, we've walked quite friendly up to Death;
　　Sat down and eaten with him, cool and bland,—
　　Pardoned his spilling mess-tins in our hand.
We've sniffed the green thick odour of his breath,—
Our eyes wept, but our courage didn't writhe.
　　He's spat at us with bullets and he's coughed
　　Shrapnel. We chorussed when he sang aloft;
We whistled while he shaved us with his scythe.

Oh, Death was never enemy of ours!
　　We laughed at him, we leagued with him, old chum.
No soldier's paid to kick against his powers.
　　We laughed, knowing that better men would come,
And greater wars; when each proud fighter brags
He wars on Death—for lives; not men—for flags.

BM has six drafts. The final draft has, subscribed to the title and cancelled, *A Postscript to Siegfried Sassoon's letter to Robert Graves, ending*—and then quotes the two lines as epigraph.
EB follows this final draft in the main, but makes a few minor alterations based on what appears to be the penultimate draft. I print the EB version except for l. 14.
l. 14: EB has *He wars on Death—for Life; not men—for flags.*
BM (a) has *He fights on Death, for lives; not men, for flags.*
BM (b) has *He wars on Death,—for lives; not men—for flags.*
Wars on is evidently preferable to *Fights on*: and *lives* avoids the slickness of *Death/Life*

OTHER POEMS, AND FRAGMENTS

The End

After the blast of lightning from the east,
The flourish of loud clouds, the Chariot Throne;
After the drums of time have rolled and ceased,
And by the bronze west long retreat is blown,

Shall Life renew these bodies? Of a truth
All death will he annul, all tears assuage?—
Or fill these void veins full again with youth,
And wash, with an immortal water, Age?

When I do ask white Age he saith not so:
"My head hangs weighed with snow."
And when I hearken to the Earth, she saith:
"My fiery heart shrinks, aching. It is death
Mine ancient scars shall not be glorified,
Nor my titanic tears, the seas, be dried."

BM has three drafts.
l. 2: BM (a) has *high* cancelled in favour of *loud*, and *the Throne,
the Chariot* cancelled in favour of *the Chariot Throne;*
l. 4: BM (b), *Space's retreat in a bronze sunset blown.*
SS, *And from the bronze west.*
l. 5: BM (a) shows *Shall* {*Life* / ~~*God* renew~~} {*these bodies* / ~~*the righteous*~~}
l. 6: EB, *Will He annul.* Owen's emendations in the previous line
indicate that he wished the Deity to be kept out of this poem.
l. 7: EB, *Fill the void veins of Life again with youth,*
l. 10: all three BM drafts have *everlasting snow*, but in the final one
everlasting has been struck out and not replaced. Though Owen
nowhere else departs from the normal length of the sonnet line, I
find the line far more effective without *everlasting*, and therefore
follow EB in printing it thus.
l. 14: EB and earlier BM drafts give *the sea*. In the final draft *sea*
was written first, then an *s* added.

The Unreturning

Suddenly night crushed out the day and hurled
Her remnants over cloud-peaks, thunder-walled.
Then fell a stillness such as harks appalled
When far-gone dead return upon the world.

There watched I for the Dead; but no ghost woke.
Each one whom Life exiled I named and called.
But they were all too far, or dumbed, or thralled,
And never one fared back to me or spoke.

Then peered the indefinite unshapen dawn
With vacant gloaming, sad as half-lit minds,
The weak-limned hour when sick men's sighs are drained.
And while I wondered on their being withdrawn,
Gagged by the smothering wing which none unbinds,
I dreaded even a heaven with doors so chained.

BM has two drafts: HO has one. I am unable to discover the source
of the EB version printed above, which differs at points from BM
and HO.

l. 1: BM has *A ponderous night*
~~Implacable~~

l. 2: BM has *The remnants of the light behind the Vald.*

ll. 5–8: BM has *I thought upon those dead, all dumb, all thralled.*
I yearned towards life's exiles, and I called,
But never one fared back to me, none spoke,
                          from his ~~sleeping~~
But not one sleeper out of ~~Hades~~ *woke.*
                    im
l. 9: BM has *Then yawned the* ~~premature~~*mature*
                    piteous
l. 10: BM has *The* ~~hopeless~~ *gloam, as sad as*

l. 11: BM has *Even the hour*

l. 12: BM has *And as I wondered on them, being withdrawn,*

l. 13: BM has *The smothering Dark, whence None unbinds,*

Miners

There was a whispering in my hearth,
    A sigh of the coal,
Grown wistful of a former earth
    It might recall.

I listened for a tale of leaves
    And smothered ferns;
Frond-forests; and the low, sly lives
    Before the fawns.

My fire might show steam-phantoms simmer
    From Time's old cauldron,
Before the birds made nests in summer,
    Or men had children.

But the coals were murmuring of their mine,
    And moans down there
Of boys that slept wry sleep, and men
    Writhing for air.

And I saw white bones in the cinder-shard.
    Bones without number;
For many hearts with coal are charred
    And few remember.

I thought of some who worked dark pits
    Of war, and died
Digging the rock where Death reputes
    Peace lies indeed.

Comforted years will sit soft-chaired
    In rooms of amber;
The years will stretch their hands, well-cheered
    By our lives' ember.

The centuries will burn rich loads
    With which we groaned,

Whose warmth shall lull their dreaming lids
    While songs are crooned.
But they will not dream of us poor lads
    Lost in the ground.

BM has one draft, a fair copy.

l. 8: probably a mis-spelling for *faurs*.

l. 19: BM has *Many the muscled bodies charred*, uncancelled, and written above it, in brackets, the present text.

l. 34: BM has *Left*, uncancelled, and below it, in brackets, *Lost*

In a letter to his mother, dated January 17, 1918, Owen wrote *I send you the Coal poem.*

Happiness

Ever again to breathe pure happiness,
The happiness our mother gave us, boys?
To smile at nothings, needing no caress?
Have we not laughed too often since with joys?
Have we not wrought too sick and sorrowful wrongs
For her hands' pardoning? The sun may cleanse,
And time, and starlight. Life will sing sweet songs,
And gods will show us pleasures more than men's.

Yet heaven looks smaller than the old doll's-home,
No nestling place is left in bluebell bloom,
And the wide arms of trees have lost their scope.
The former happiness is unreturning:
Boys' griefs are not so grievous as our yearning,
Boys have no sadness sadder than our hope.

BM has one draft; HO has one. A third draft, presented by the
poet's mother, is in the Bodleian Library.
ll. 1–2: HO (dated Feb., 1917), gives

> *Ever to know unhoping happiness,*
> *Harboured in heaven, being a Mother's boy.*

The last phrase was doubtless too confessional for the poet's liking.
l. 6: EB has *their hands'*: BM and Bodleian both have *her hands'*
ll. 9–14: I prefer these lines, from the BM draft, to the Bodleian
draft as printed by EB:—

> *But the old Happiness is unreturning.*
> *Boy's griefs are not so grievous as youth's yearning,*
> *Boys have no sadness sadder than our hope.*
> *We who have seen the gods' kaleidoscope,*
> *And played with human passions for our toys,*
> *We know men suffer chiefly by their joys.*

l. 9: The end of this line is heavily emended: another possible read-
ing would be *Yet heaven looks smaller than the old doll's-house rooms*:
the next line could be deciphered as ending with *bluebell blooms*,
l. 13: Bodleian has sestet as printed in note above, but with *human*
and *vital* deleted, and *fragile* substituted.
In a letter to his mother, dated February 25, 1917, Owen says that
he has finished this poem.

Shadwell Stair

I am the ghost of Shadwell Stair.
　　Along the wharves by the water-house,
　　And through the dripping slaughter-house,
I am the shadow that walks there.

Yet I have flesh both firm and cool,
　　And eyes tumultuous as the gems
　　Of moons and lamps in the lapping Thames
When dusk sails wavering down the pool.

Shuddering the purple street-arc burns
　　Where I watch always; from the banks
　　Dolorously the shipping clanks,
And after me a strange tide turns.

I walk till the stars of London wane
　　And dawn creeps up the Shadwell Stair.
　　But when the crowing syrens blare
I with another ghost am lain.

BM has two drafts.
l. 7: BM (a) gives *the full Thames*

Six o'clock in Princes Street

In twos and threes, they have not far to roam,
  Crowds that thread eastward, gay of eyes;
Those seek no further than their quiet home,
  Wives, walking westward, slow and wise.

Neither should I go fooling over clouds,
  Following gleams unsafe, untrue,
And tiring after beauty through star-crowds,
  Dared I go side by side with you;

Or be you in the gutter where you stand,
  Pale rain-flawed phantom of the place,
With news of all the nations in your hand,
  And all their sorrows in your face.

BM has one draft. HO has the following prose notes for the poem:—

Princes St., Edinburgh
The Sunday crowd, by families and couples,
Enjoy the air.   *They are resigned to war*
For them the war is but a chalking of the pavement.
Gas-driven busses
                sugarless tea   enslavement
But plenty of handsome men in kilts and trews

l. 9: EB gives *on the gutter*

The Roads Also

The roads also have their wistful rest,
When the weathercocks perch still and roost,
And the town is a candle-lit room—
The streets also dream their dream.

The old houses muse of the old days
And their fond trees leaning on them doze,
On their steps chatter and clatter stops,
On their doors a strange hand taps.

Men remember alien ardours
As the dusk unearths old mournful odours.
In the garden unborn child souls wail
And the dead scribble on walls.

Though their own child cry for them in tears,
Women weep but hear no sound upstairs.
They believe in loves they had not lived
And in passion past the reach of the stairs
    To the world's towers or stars.

BM has two drafts, both untitled and tentative, conflated by EB
for the present text.
l. 3: EB retained a cancelled *quiet like* before *a candle-lit room*
ll. 9–12: One BM draft has here—

> *They remember alien ardours and far futures*
> *And the smiles not seen in happy features.*
> *Their begetters call them from the gutters.*
> *In the gardens unborn child-souls wail,*
>   *And the dead scribble on walls.*

Hospital Barge at Cérisy

Budging the sluggard ripples of the Somme,
A barge round old Cérisy slowly slewed.
Softly her engines down the current screwed
And chuckled in her, with contented hum.

Till fairy tinklings struck their croonings dumb.
The waters rumpling at the stern subdued.
The lock-gate took her bulging amplitude.
Gently from out the gurgling lock she swum.

One reading by that sunset raised his eyes
To watch her lessening westward quietly,
Till, as she neared the bend, her funnel screamed.

And that long lamentation made him wise
How unto Avalon, in agony,
Kings passed in the dark barge, which Merlin dreamed.

December 8, 1917.

BM has three drafts; HO has one.
l. 8: HO and earlier BM drafts give *gently into*, which EB follows.
The final BM draft has *into* deleted and *from out* inserted. I prefer
this, as a new stage in the barge's progress, to the EB text, which
makes the line a repetition of the previous line's meaning.

Training

Not this week nor this month dare I lie down
In languor under lime trees or smooth smile.
Love must not kiss my face pale that is brown.

My lips, parting, shall drink space, mile by mile;
Strong meats be all my hunger; my renown
Be the clean beauty of speed and pride of style.

Cold winds encountered on the racing Down
Shall thrill my heated bareness; but awhile
None else may meet me till I wear my crown.

June 1918.

BM has one draft.
l. 4: *parting* could be read as *panting* in the MS. The latter suits the
theme of running; the former fits better the metaphor of *shall drink
space*.

Sonnet

TO A CHILD

Sweet is your antique body, not yet young.
Beauty withheld from youth that looks for youth.
Fair only for your father. Dear among
Masters in art. To all men else uncouth
Save me, who know your smile comes very old,
Learnt of the happy dead that laughed with gods;
For earlier suns than ours have lent you gold,
Sly fauns and trees have given you jigs and nods.

But soon your heart, hot-beating like a bird's,
Shall slow down. Youth shall lop your hair,
And you must learn wry meanings in our words.
Your smile shall dull, because too keen aware;
And when for hopes your hand shall be uncurled,
Your eyes shall close, being opened to the world.

BM has one draft, and some notes for the poem.
l. 8: BM, *fawns*: the sense of the preceding lines suggest that this
is a mis-spelling. See also p. 91, l. 8, where *fawns* is probably a mis-
spelling for *fauns*.
l. 14: EB, *open*

To Eros

In that I loved you, Love, I worshipped you.
In that I worshipped well, I sacrificed.
All of most worth I bound and burnt and slew:
Old peaceful lives; frail flowers; firm friends; and Christ.

I slew all falser loves; I slew all true,
That I might nothing love but your truth, Boy.
Fair fame I cast away as bridegrooms do
Their wedding garments in their haste of joy.

But when I fell upon your sandalled feet,
You laughed; you loosed away my lips; you rose.
I heard the singing of your wings' retreat;
Far-flown, I watched you flush the Olympian snows,
Beyond my hoping. Starkly I returned
To stare upon the ash of all I burned.

BM has two drafts.
ll. 1–3: both BM drafts give punctuation as above. EB gives

> In that I loved you, Love, I worshipped you,
> In that I worshipped well, I sacrificed
> All of most worth. I bound and burnt and slew
> Old peaceful lives; frail flowers; firm friends; and Christ.

l. 4: BM (b) has *The innocent small things, far friends and Christ.*

My Shy Hand

My shy hand shades a hermitage apart,
   O large enough for thee, and thy brief hours.
Life there is sweeter held than in God's heart,
   Stiller than in the heavens of hollow flowers.

The wine is gladder there than in gold bowls.
   And Time shall not drain thence, nor trouble spill.
Sources between my fingers feed all souls,
   Where thou mayest cool thy lips, and draw thy fill.

Five cushions hath my hand, for reveries;
   And one deep pillow for thy brow's fatigues;
Languor of June all winterlong, and ease
   For ever from the vain untravelled leagues.

Thither your years may gather in from storm,
And Love, that sleepeth there, will keep thee warm.

BM has three drafts and one part-draft. LG has one draft, entitled
Sonnet to Beauty, and dated *Aug. 29–30, 1917.*
ll. 1–2: an early draft gives

> *You hold in your pure hand a world apart*
> *O large enough for me, and my brief hours!*

ll. 5–8: LG has

> *The wine is deeper there than in life's bowls;*
> *And Time shall not spill there; nor Equity*
> *Weigh there; for sense shall still our swaying souls;*
> *And odours drape a sleep o'er Memory.*

The Kind Ghosts

She sleeps on soft, last breaths; but no ghost looms
Out of the stillness of her palace wall,
Her wall of boys on boys and dooms on dooms.

She dreams of golden gardens and sweet glooms,
Not marvelling why her roses never fall
Nor what red mouths were torn to make their blooms.

The shades keep down which well might roam her hall.
Quiet their blood lies in her crimson rooms
And she is not afraid of their footfall.

They move not from her tapestries, their pall,
Nor pace her terraces, their hecatombs,
Lest aught she be disturbed, or grieved at all.

July 30, 1918.

BM has one draft, heavily marked to indicate alliteration and
internal rhyming. In stanza 1, *s, st, l* and *d* are thus marked; in
stanza 2, *g, n, m, golden* and *roses, dreams* and *sweet*; in stanza 3,
shades and *afraid, quiet* and *crimson, afraid* and *footfall*; in stanza 4,
p and *t*.

Winter Song

The browns, the olives, and the yellows died,
And were swept up to heaven; where they glowed
Each dawn and set of sun till Christmastide,
And when the land lay pale for them, pale-snowed,
Fell back, and down the snow-drifts flamed and flowed.

From off your face, into the winds of winter,
The sun-brown and the summer-gold are blowing;
But they shall gleam again with spiritual glinter,
When paler beauty on your brows falls snowing,
And through those snows my looks shall be soft-going.

October 18, 1917.

BM has four drafts.
l. 8: *sudden* and *rosy* are cancelled in favour of *spiritual*.

Music

I have been urged by earnest violins
And drunk their mellow sorrows to the slake
Of all my sorrows and my thirsting sins.
My heart has beaten for a brave drum's sake.
Huge chords have wrought me mighty: I have hurled
Thuds of God's thunder. And with old winds pondered
Over the curse of this chaotic world,—
With low lost winds that maundered as they wandered.

I have been gay with trivial fifes that laugh;
And songs more sweet than possible things are sweet;
And gongs, and oboes. Yet I guessed not half
Life's symphony till I had made hearts beat,
And touched Love's body into trembling cries,
And blown my love's lips into laughs and sighs.

October 1916–1917.

BM has five drafts: HO has one draft, on the reverse of a draft
letter from Craiglockhart.
This poem is an interesting example of Owen's occasional regres-
sion, even at this late date, into his earlier, lush way of writing. The
last two lines are obviously influenced by Keats: lines 1–3 are
Ninety-ish: 1. 10 might have been written by Rupert Brooke: but
lines 6–9 have the movement and language of the mature Owen. The
number of attempts he made at this poem, over a considerable
period, reveal his uncertainty and uneasiness in the task of ab-
sorbing his influences.
l. 12: EB has *Life's sympathy.*

Storm

His face was charged with beauty as a cloud
   With glimmering lightning. When it shadowed me
   I shook, and was uneasy as a tree
That draws the brilliant danger, tremulous, bowed.

So must I tempt that face to loose its lightning.
   Great gods, whose beauty is death, will laugh above,
   Who made his beauty lovelier than love.
I shall be bright with their unearthly brightening.

And happier were it if my sap consume;
Glorious will shine the opening of my heart;
The land shall freshen that was under gloom;
What matter if all men cry aloud and start,
And women hide bleak faces in their shawl,
At those hilarious thunders of my fall?

October 1916.

BM has one draft, a fair copy.
l. 8: here, in a relatively immature poem, is a line foreshadowing
Owen's mature style.

To My Friend

(WITH AN IDENTITY DISC)

If ever I had dreamed of my dead name
 High in the heart of London, unsurpassed
By Time for ever, and the Fugitive, Fame,
 There seeking a long sanctuary at last,—

Or if I onetime hoped to hide its shame,
—Shame of success, and sorrow of defeats,—
Under those holy cypresses, the same
 That shade always the quiet place of Keats,

Now rather thank I God there is no risk
 Of gravers scoring it with florid screed.
Let my inscription be this soldier's disc. . . .
 Wear it, sweet friend. Inscribe no date nor deed.
But may thy heart-beat kiss it, night and day,
Until the name grow blurred and fade away.

BM has five drafts. I follow the EB text, which is largely a confla-
tion of two of these drafts.
l. 2: two drafts have a reference here to Westminster—Poet's
Corner is implied.
l. 11: this line evidently gave Owen great trouble. EB's version is
clearly preferable to any of those in the consecutive BM drafts (e.g.
But let my death be memoried on this disc): it is to be found on a
separate folio, where the following lines have been jotted down—

> *Well, here's a meeter tombstone; and no risk*
>
> *Of mason's marring it with* { *florid*
> {*ill-scored* screeds.
>
> *For let my inscription be this soldier's disc.*

An early draft of this poem appears in a letter to Owen's brother,
Colin. The poet says that he *started it yesterday*: the letter is dated
March 24, (1917).

> *If ever I had dreamed of my dead name*
> *High in the heart of London; unsurpassed*

By Time forever; and the fugitive, Fame,
There taking a long sanctuary at last,
—I'll better that. Yea, now, I think with shame
How once I wished it hidd'n from its defeats
Under those holy cypresses, the same
That mourn around the quiet place of Keats.

Now rather let's be thankful there's no risk
Of gravers scoring it with hideous screed.
For let my gravestone be this body-disc
Which was my yoke. Inscribe no date, nor deed.
But let thy heart-beat kiss it night and day . . .
Until the name grow vague and wear away.

Fragment: Not one Corner . . .

Not one corner of a foreign field
But a span as wide as Europe,
Deep as (   ).
I looked and saw.
An appearance of a titan's grave,
And the length thereof a thousand miles.
It crossed all Europe like a mystic road,
Or as the Spirits' Pathway lieth on the night.
And I heard a voice crying,
This is the Path of Glory.

This BM fragment was printed by EB in his notes. It is all that
Owen completed of a poem to be called *An Imperial Elegy* or
Libretto for Marche Funèbre.

Fragment:
Cramped in that Funnelled Hole

Cramped in that funnelled hole, they watched the dawn
Open a jagged rim around; a yawn
Of death's jaws, which had all but swallowed them
Stuck in the bottom of his throat of phlegm.

They were in one of many mouths of Hell
Not seen of seers in visions; only felt
As teeth of traps; when bones and the dead are smelt
Under the mud where long ago they fell
Mixed with the sour sharp odour of the shell.

BM has three attempts at this poem on a single folio: each is
heavily corrected, but none cancelled. I follow EB in printing the
third of these drafts.
l. 4: EB, *middle*
l. 5: BM has a variant, printed in brackets by EB, *And they
remembered Hell has many mouths*

Fragment:
I saw his Round Mouth's Crimson . . .

I saw his round mouth's crimson deepen as it fell,
   Like a Sun, in his last deep hour;
Watched the magnificent recession of farewell,
   Clouding, half gleam, half glower,
And a last splendour burn the heavens of his cheek.
   And in his eyes
The cold stars lighting, very old and bleak,
   In different skies.

BM has one draft, untitled.

Fragment:
As Bronze may be much Beautified

As bronze may be much beautified
By lying in the dark damp soil,
So men who fade in dust of warfare fade
Fairer, and sorrow blooms their soul.

Like pearls which noble women wear
And, tarnishing, awhile confide
Unto the old salt sea to feed,
Many return more lustrous than they were.

But what of them buried profound,
Buried where we can no more find,
Who [   ]
Lie dark for ever under abysmal war?

BM has one draft, untitled.

Has Your Soul Sipped?

Has your soul sipped
    Of the sweetness of all sweets?
Has it well supped
    But yet hungers and sweats?

I have been witness
    Of a strange sweetness,
All fancy surpassing
    Past all supposing.

Passing the rays
    Of the rubies of morning,
Or the soft rise
    Of the moon; or the meaning
Known to the rose
    Of her mystery and mourning.

Sweeter than nocturnes
    Of the wild nightingale
Or than love's nectar
    After life's gall.

Sweeter than odours
    Of living leaves,
Sweeter than ardours
    Of dying loves.

Sweeter than death
    And dreams hereafter
To one in dearth
    Of life and its laughter.

Or the proud wound
    The victor wears
Or the last end
    Of all wars.

Or the sweet murder
    After long guard
Unto the martyr
    Smiling at God;

To me was that Smile,
    Faint as a wan, worn myth,
Faint and exceeding small,
    On a boy's murdered mouth.

Though from his throat
    The life-tide leaps
There was no threat
    On his lips.

But with the bitter blood
    And the death-smell
All his life's sweetness bled
    Into a smile.

HO has one draft.
On the reverse of the last folio, the poet jotted down *Marlboro' and Other Poems/Chas Sorely* [sic]. Sorley's book was published in January, 1916. If Owen noted this title within a few months after its publication, it would indicate that the poem above was an early experiment in consonantal rhyme.
The fragment given below was printed separately in EB, and appears to be a later version of certain stanzas in the above.

It is not death
    Without hereafter
To one in dearth
    Of life and its laughter,

Nor the sweet murder
    Dealt slow and even
Unto the martyr
    Smiling at heaven:

It is the smile
    Faint as a [waning] myth,

Faint, and exceeding small
On a boy's murdered mouth.

MINOR POEMS, AND JUVENILIA

From My Diary, July 1914

Leaves
    Murmuring by myriads in the shimmering trees.
Lives
    Wakening with wonder in the Pyrenees.
Birds
    Cheerily chirping in the early day.
Bards
    Singing of summer, scything thro' the hay.
Bees
    Shaking the heavy dews from bloom and frond.
Boys
    Bursting the surface of the ebony pond.
Flashes
    Of swimmers carving thro' the sparkling cold.
Fleshes
    Gleaming with wetness to the morning gold.
A mead
    Bordered about with warbling water brooks.
A maid
    Laughing the love-laugh with me; proud of looks.
The heat
    Throbbing between the upland and the peak.
Her heart
    Quivering with passion to my pressèd cheek.
Braiding
    Of floating flames across the mountain brow.
Brooding
    Of stillness; and a sighing of the bough.
Stirs
    Of leaflets in the gloom; soft petal-showers;
Stars
    Expanding with the starr'd nocturnal flowers.

BM has one draft.
This poem is the earliest finished example of Owen's use of consonantal rhyming.

ll. 1–2: BM has uncancelled variant, *Leaves/Drenched in mist: mist on the Pyrenees.*
ll. 3–4: deleted in BM.
l. 10: BM, *blooms*

On My Songs

Though unseen Poets, many and many a time,
Have answered me as if they knew my woe,
And it might seem have fashioned so their rime
To be my own soul's cry; easing the flow
Of my dumb tears with language sweet as sobs,
Yet are there days when all these hoards of thought
Hold nothing for me. Not one verse that throbs
Throbs with my head, or as my brain is fraught.

'Tis then I voice mine own weird reveries:
Low croonings of a motherless child, in gloom
Singing his frightened self to sleep, are these.
One night, if thou shouldst lie in this Sick Room
Dreading the Dark thou darest not illume;
Listen; my voice may haply lend thee ease.

BM has one draft: HO has one, dated Jan. 4, 1913.
ll. 6–8 are significant as expressing, at this early date, Owen's
occasional dissatisfaction with the traditional poetry which so
powerfully influenced him.

Antaeus: A Fragment

So neck to stubborn neck, and obstinate knee to knee,
Wrestled those two; and peerless Heracles
Could not prevail, nor get at any vantage . . .
So those huge hands that, small, had snapped great snakes,
Let slip the writhing of Antaeus' wrists:
Those hero's hands that wrenched the necks of bulls,
Now fumbled round the slim Antaeus' limbs,
Baffled. Then anger swelled in Heracles,
And terribly he grappled broader arms,
And yet more firmly fixed his graspéd feet.
And up his back the muscles bulged and shone
Like climbing banks and domes of towering cloud.
And they who watched that wrestling say he laughed,
But not so loud as on Eurystheus of old.

HO has one draft, sent by the poet to his mother in a letter dated
July 17, 1917. Owen spells *Antaeas* throughout.
In a letter to Leslie Gunston, dated *Wednesday, July, 1917*, Owen
said, *Last week I wrote (to order) a strong bit of Blank: on Antaeas
v. Heracles. These are the best lines, methinks (N.B. Antaeas deriving
strength from his Mother Earth nearly licked old Herk).*—

. . . How Earth herself empowered him with her touch,
  Gave him the grip and stringency of 'Winter,
  And all the ardour of th' invincible Spring;
  How all the blood of June glutted his heart,
  And all the glow of huge autumnal storms
  Stirred on his face, and flickered from his eyes.

The Promisers

When I awoke, the glancing day looked gay;
The air said: Fare you fleetly; you will meet him !
And when the prosp'rous sun was well begun,
I heard a bird say: Sweetly you shall greet him!

The sun fell strong and bold upon my shoulder;
It hung, it clung as it were my friend's arm.
The birds fifed on before, shrill-piping pipers,
Right down to town; and there they ceased to charm.

And there I wandered till the noon came soon,
And chimed: The time is hastening with his face!
Sly twilight said: I bring him; wait till late!
But darkness harked forlorn to my lone pace.

BM has one draft, on Craiglockhart War Hospital writing-paper.
l. 5: EB, *felt*

The Fates

They watch me, those informers to the Fates,
Called Fortune, Chance, Necessity, and Death;
Time, in disguise as one who serves and waits,
Eternity, as girls of fragrant breath.
I know them. Men and Boys are in their pay,
And those I hold my trustiest friends may prove
Agents of Theirs to take me if I stray
From fatal ordinance. If I move they move,—

Escape? There is one unwatched way: your eyes,
O Beauty! Keep me good that secret gate!
And when the cordon tightens of the spies
Let the close iris of your eyes grow great.
So I'll evade the vice and rack of age
And miss the march of lifetime, stage by stage.

BM has one draft, with *2nd Draught* written beside the title. LG
has one draft.
l. 9: BM, *ordnance.*
ll. 1–2: LG, *They watch me, shadowing, to inform the Fates,*
                   Those constables called Fortune, Chance, and Death;
l. 13: LG,   *So I'll evade the press-gang raid of age*
The LG draft is dated by the poet *June 2, '17.* This date is printed
in EB. But, in his letter to Leslie Gunston, which is headed Craig-
lockhart War Hospital/*July 1, 1917,* the poet wrote *Late last
night I very hastily draughted a Fate sonnet,* and writes out this
sonnet below, with (*2nd Draught*) beside the title. Evidently his
dating of *June 2, '17* was a slip of memory.

This is the Track

This is the track my life is setting on,
    Spacious the spanless way I wend;
The blackness of darkness may be held for me?
    And barren plunging without end?

Why dare I fear? For other wandering souls
    Burn thro' the night of that far bourne.
And they are light unto themselves; and aureoles
    Self-radiated there are worn.

And when in after-times we make return
    Round solar bounds awhile to run,
They gather many satellites astern
    And turn aside the very sun.

BM has one draft, and one part-draft. See next page for another
version of this poem.

O World of many Worlds

O World of many Worlds; O life of lives,
    What centre hast thou? Where am I?
O whither is it thy fierce onrush drives?
    Fight I, or drift; or stand or fly?

The loud machinery spins, thy work in touch;
    Wheels whirl in systems, zone in zone.
I myself, having sometime moved with such,
    Would strike a centre of mine own.

Lend hand, O Fate, for I am down, am lost!
    Fainting by violence of the Dance . . .
Ah thanks, I stand—the floor is crossed,
    And I am where but few advance.

I see men far below me where they swarm . . .
    Haply above me—be it so!
Does space to compass-points confirm,
    And can we say a star stands high or low?

Not more complex the millions of the stars
    Than are the hearts of mortal brothers;
As far remote as Neptune from small Mars
    Is one man's nature from another's.

But all hold course unalterably fixed;
    They follow destinies foreplanned:
I envy not these lives their faith unmixed,
    I would not step with such a band.

To be a meteor, fast, eccentric, lone,
    Lawless; in passage through all spheres,
Warning the earth of wider ways unknown
    And rousing men with heavenly fears—

This is the track reserved for my endeavour;
    Spanless the erring way I wend.

Blackness of darkness is my meed for ever?
　　And barren plunging without end?

O glorious fear! Those other wandering souls
　　High burning through that outer bourne
Are lights unto themselves. Fair aureoles
　　Self-radiated there are worn.

And when in after times those stars return
　　And strike once more earth's horizon,
They gather many satellites astern,
　　For they are greater than this system's sun.

BM has one draft.
This poem, with its faint echoes both of Shelley and Hardy, is
chiefly interesting for being so much at variance, in thought and
language, with the bulk of Owen's immature work.

Song of Songs

Sing me at morn but only with your laugh;
Even as Spring that laugheth into leaf;
Even as Love that laugheth after Life.

Sing me but only with your speech all day,
As voluble leaflets do; let viols die;
The least word of your lips is melody!

Sing me at eve but only with your sigh!
Like lifting seas it solaceth; breathe so,
Slowly and low, the sense that no songs say.

Sing me at midnight with your murmurous heart!
Let youth's immortal-moaning chords be heard
Throbbing through you, and sobbing, unsubdued.

This is the form in which the poem appeared in the Craiglockhart
magazine, under Owen's editorship. BM has a draft, considerably
emended, which differs in some respects from the above.
The poem is interesting as an example of Owen's relapse into the
'poetic' manner of his juvenilia.

All Sounds have been as Music

All sounds have been as music to my listening:
    Pacific lamentations of slow bells,
The crunch of boots on blue snow rosy-glistening,
    Shuffle of autumn leaves; and all farewells:

Bugles that sadden all the evening air,
    And country bells clamouring their last appeals
Before [the] music of the evening prayer;
    Bridges, sonorous under carriage wheels.

Gurgle of sluicing surge through hollow rocks,
    The gluttonous lapping of the waves on weeds,
Whisper of grass; the myriad-tinkling flocks,
    The warbling drawl of flutes and shepherds' reeds.

The orchestral noises of October nights
    Blowing [   ] symphonetic storms
Of startled clarions [   ]
    Drums, rumbling and rolling thunderous and [ ].

Thrilling of throstles in the keen blue dawn,
    Bees fumbling and fuming over sainfoin-fields.

BM has one draft, untitled. This poem, and the one printed on the next page, appear to be two attempts at a single poem.
l. 11: EB, *grasses*
l. 17: EB, *clear blue*

Bugles Sang

Bugles sang, saddening the evening air,
And bugles answered, sorrowful to hear.

Voices of boys were by the river-side.
Sleep mothered them; and left the twilight sad.
The shadow of the morrow weighed on men.

Voices of old despondency resigned,
Bowed by the shadow of the morrow, slept.

[   ] dying tone
Of receding voices that will not return.
The wailing of the high far-travelling shells
And the deep cursing of the provoking [   ].

The monstrous anger of our taciturn guns.
The majesty of the insults of their mouths.

BM has one draft, untitled.

1914

War broke: and now the Winter of the world
With perishing great darkness closes in.
The foul tornado, centred at Berlin,
Is over all the width of Europe whirled,
Rending the sails of progress. Rent or furled
Are all Art's ensigns. Verse wails. Now begin
Famines of thought and feeling. Love's wine's thin.
The grain of human Autumn rots, down-hurled.

For after Spring had bloomed in early Greece,
And Summer blazed her glory out with Rome,
An Autumn softly fell, a harvest home,
A slow grand age, and rich with all increase.
But now, for us, wild Winter, and the need
Of sowings for new Spring, and blood for seed.

BM has two drafts, one entitled *The Seed* and dated *1914*. HO has
two drafts. The poem is of interest both for its resemblances and
its unlikenesses to the state of mind expressed in Rupert Brooke's
1914.
l. 3: BM (b), *The cylone of the pressure on Berlin*
l. 8: BM (b), *earth's great autumn*
l. 10: BM (b), *blazed to perfect strength*
ll. 11–12: BM (b), *There fell a slow grand age, a harvest home,*
                Quietly ripening, ~~rich with all increase~~.
l. 13: BM (b), *But now the exigent winter*

The One Remains

I sometimes think of those pale, perfect faces
My wonder has not looked upon, as yet;
And of those others never to be met;
And often pore I on the secret traces
Left in my heart, of countenances seen,
And lost as soon as seen,—but which mine eye
Remembers as my old home, or the lie
Of landscapes whereupon my windows lean.

And as for those long known and worshipped long,
But now, alas! no longer, and the song
Of voices that have said 'Adieu, we part,'
Their reminiscences would cease my heart,
Except I still hoped find, some time, some place,
All beauty, once for ever, in one face.

BM has one draft: HO has three drafts.

To the Bitter Sweet-heart: a Dream

One evening Eros took me by the hand,
  And having folded feathers round my head,
Or sleep like feathers, towards a far hope sped,
  I groping, for he bade me understand
He would soon fill with Your's my other hand.
But when I heard his singing wings expand
  My face fell deeply in his shoulder.
  Sweet moons we flew thus, yet I waned not older
But in his exquisiteness I flagged, unmanned
Till, when his wings were drooping to an end,
Feeling my empty hand fulfilled with His,
I knew Love gave himself my passion-friend.
So my old quest of you requited is,
Ampler than e'er I asked of your girl's grace.
I shall not ask you more, nor see your face.

LG has one draft.

The Sleeping Beauty

Sojourning through a southern realm in youth,
I came upon a house by happy chance
Where bode a marvellous Beauty. There, romance
Flew faerily until I lit on truth—
For lo! the fair Child slumbered. Though, forsooth,
She lay not blanketed in drowsy trance,
But leapt alert of limb and keen of glance,
From sun to shower; from gaiety to ruth;
Yet breathed her loveliness asleep in her:
For, when I kissed, her eyelids knew no stir.
So back I drew tiptoe from that Princess,
Because it was too soon, and not my part,
To start voluptuous pulses in her heart,
And kiss her to the world of Consciousness.

BM has one draft: HO has four drafts.
I have included this poem for the sake of the last four lines, which
reveal something important about the young Owen's temperament
or state of mind.

Sonnet Autumnal

If it be very strange and sorrowful
To scent the first night-frost in autumntide:
If on the sombre day when Summer died
Men shuddered, awed to hear her burial:
And if the dissolution of one rose
(Whereof the future holds unnumbered store)
Engender human tears,—ah! how much more
Sorrows and suffers he whose sense foreknows
The weakening and the withering of a love,
The dying of a love that had been dear!
Who feels upon a hand, but late love-warm,
A hardness of indifference, like a glove;
And in the dead calm of a voice may hear
The menace of a drear and mighty storm.

BM has two drafts: HO has one draft, with title deleted.
l. 3: BM (b) *moaning eve*
l. 6: BM (b) *abundant store*
Though its thought and expression are conventional, this early
poem shows promise in its command of legato and elaborate
syntax.

Long Ages Past

Long ages past in Egypt thou wert worshipped
And thou wert wrought from ivory and beryl.
They brought thee jewels and they brought their slain,
Thy feet were dark with blood of sacrifice.
From dawn to midnight, O my painted idol,
Thou satest smiling, and the noise of killing
Was harp and timbrel in thy pale jade ears:
The livid dead were given thee for toys.

*　　　*　　　*

Thou wert a mad slave in a Persian palace,
And the King loved thee for thy furious beauty,
And all men heard thy ravings with a smile
Because thy face was fairer than a flower.
But with a little knife so wantonly
Thou slewest women and thy pining lovers,
And on thy lips the stain of crimson blood,
And on thy brow the pallor of their death.

*　　　*　　　*

Thou art the dream beheld by frenzied princes
In smoke of opium—thou art the last fulfilment
Of all the wicked, and of all the beautiful.
We hold thee as a poppy to our mouths,
Finding with thee forgetfulness of God.
Thou art the face reflected in a mirror
Of wild desire, of pain, of bitter pleasure.
The witches shout thy name beneath the moon,
The fires of Hell have held thee in their fangs.

OS has one draft, dated *31.X.14.* I have corrected punctuation and
some odd mis-spellings, e.g. *wumen, whitches.*

Purple

Vividly gloomy, with bright darkling glows
Of fine stars, or night-sparkling southern shores;
Stain of strong fruits, wines, passions, and the cores
Of all quick hearts! Yet from its deepness blows
Aroma and romance of violets;
Softness of far land, lost; pacific lift
Of smoke through quiet trees; and that wild drift
Of smoulder where the flame of evening sets.
Yea, that columnar, thunder-throning cloud
Wears it so stately that therein the King
Stands before men, and lies in death's hands, proud.
Purest, it is a diamond dawn of Spring,
And yet the Veil of Venus and youth's skin
Mauve-marbled; purpling young Love's mouth for sacred sin.

BM has two drafts: HO has one draft.
l. 9: for *that*, BM has *those*, which is impossible because of *cloud wears*.
l. 10: the last word of this line is illegible, except for a *g* at the end; but rhyme and sense suggest that it is *King*.

Maundy Thursday

Between the brown hands of a server-lad
The silver cross was offered to be kissed.
The men came up, lugubrious, but not sad,
And knelt reluctantly, half-prejudiced.
(And kissing, kissed the emblem of a creed.)
Then mourning women knelt; meek mouths they had,
(And kissed the Body of the Christ indeed.)
Young children came, with eager lips and glad.
(These kissed a silver doll, immensely bright.)
Then I, too, knelt before that acolyte.
Above the crucifix I bent my head:
The Christ was thin, and cold, and very dead:
And yet I bowed, yea, kissed—my lips did cling
(I kissed the warm live hand that held the thing.)

BM has one draft.
It is a pity we cannot date this poem with any certainty, for it has
an edge of truthfulness, an unconventionality, and a self-revelation
which make it the most impressive of Owen's juvenilia. The last
five lines suggest it may have been written at the end of his
Dunsden period when Owen lost his belief in orthodox Christianity
and was moving towards the warm humanism that distinguishes
his mature poetry.

To——

Three rompers run together, hand in hand.
The middle boy stops short, the others hurtle:
What bumps, what shrieks, what laughter turning turtle.
Love, racing between us two, has planned
A sudden mischief: shortly he will stand
And we shall shock. We cannot help but fall;
What matter? Why, it will not hurt at all,
Our youth is supple, and the world is sand.

Better our lips should bruise our eyes, than He,
Rude love, out-run our breath; you pant, and I,
I cannot run much farther; mind that we
Both laugh with love; and having tumbled, try
To go forever children, hand in hand.
The sea is rising . . . and the world is sand.

May 10, 1916.
London.

BM has one draft.
l. 4: BM gives {~~For~~ *So* Love,} {*racing* ~~that races~~} . . .
l. 14: BM has *sea* and *wash*, both cancelled.

Spells and Incantation (a Fragment)

A vague pearl, a wan pearl
You showed me once: I peered through far-gone winters
Until my mind was fog-bound in that gem.

Blue diamonds, cold diamonds
You shook before me, so that out of them
Glittered and glowed vast diamond dawns of spring.

Tiger-eyed rubies, wrathful rubies
You rolled. I watched their hot hearts fling
Flames from each glaring summer of my life.

Quiet amber, mellow amber
You lifted; and behold the whole air rife
With evening, and the auburn autumn cloud. . . .

These are the opening stanzas of an unfinished poem. BM has six
pages of drafts and part-drafts, including some further stanzas
which are markedly inferior to those I have printed.

The Imbecile

The imbecile with long light hair, so light
That in the moon it shineth white;
The imbecile with fair long hair, so long
It falleth all her length along,
　　　She nothing knoweth of her wrong.

The imbecile with large green eyes, so clear
Therein her strange soul's deeps appear;
The imbecile with large clear eyes, so green
You see her very dreams between,
　　　Foldeth her angel hands serene.

BM has one draft, with *Problems A* written above the title. HO
has one draft, and another draft in French, with a list of consonantal
rhymes on the reverse.
This poem was possibly written during the Dunsden period: cf.
Preface, p. 16.

Beauty

The beautiful, the fair, the elegant,
Is that which pleases us, says Kant,
Without a thought of interest or advantage.

I used to watch men when they spoke of beauty
And measure their enthusiasm. One,
An old man, seeing a (   ) setting sun
Praised it (   ) a certain sense of duty
To the calm evening and his time of life.
I know another man that never says a Beauty
But of a horse;

*   *   *

Men seldom speak of beauty, beauty as such,
Not even lovers think about it much.
Women of course consider it for hours
In mirrors;

*   *   *

BM has one draft, together with a page of attempts at further lines.
I print a version of the latter below: Owen intended the culmination
of the poem to be the beauty of getting a flesh wound serious
enough to send one back to 'Blighty'.

A shrapnel ball
Just where the wet skin glistened when he swam.
Like a full-opened sea-anemone.
We both said 'What a beauty! What a beauty, lad!'
I knew that in that flower he saw a hope
Of living on, and seeing again the roses of his home.
Beauty is that which pleases and delights,
Not bringing personal advantage—Kant.
But later on I heard
A canker worked into that crimson flower
And that he sank with it
And laid it with the anemones off Dover.

Bold Horatius

Having, with bold Horatius, stamped her feet
And waved a final swashing arabesque
O'er the brave days of old, she ceased to bleat,
Slapped her Macaulay back upon the desk,
Resumed her calm gaze and her lofty seat.

There, while she heard the classic lines repeat,
Once more the teacher's face clenched stern;
For through the window, looking on the street,
Three soldiers hailed her. She made no return.
One was called 'Orace whom she would not greet.

BM has two drafts.
l. 2: EB gives *fisty arabesque*: BM (b) has *fisty* deleted.

Elegy in April and September

(jabbered among the trees)

Hush, thrush!
Hush, missen-thrush, I listen . . .
I heard the flush of footsteps through the loose leaves,
And a low whistle by the water's brim.

Be still, daffodil!
And wave me not so bravely.
Your gay gold lily daunts me and deceives,
Who follow gleams more golden and more slim.

Look, brook!
O run and look, O run!
The vain reeds shook . . . Yet search till gray sea heaves,
And I will wind among these fields for him.

Gaze, daisy!
Stare up through haze and glare,
And mark the hazardous stars all dawns and eves,
For my eye withers, and his star wanes dim.

BM has two drafts of this poem, one entitled *Ode to a Poet reported Missing: later reported Killed.* HO has one draft. I print the first four stanzas only: the remaining three are markedly inferior.

To a Comrade in Flanders

Seeing we never spied frail Fairyland,
  Though small we crouched by bluebells, moon by moon,
And are too late for Lethe's tide; too soon
  For that new bridge that leaves old Styx half-spanned:
Nor meekly unto Mecca caravanned;
  Nor bugled Asgard, skilled in magic rune;
Nor yearned for far Nirvana, the sweet swoon;
  And are from Paradise cursed out and banned:

Let's die back to those hearths we died for. Thus
Shall we be gods there. Death shall be no sev'rance.
In dull, dim chancels, flower new shrines for us.
For us, rough knees of boys shall ache with rev'rance;
For girls' breasts are the clear white Acropole
Where our own mothers' tears shall heal us whole.

Sept. 1916.

BM has three drafts. LG has one draft, entitled *A New Heaven*/(*To —on Active Service.*) The sonnet shows Owen at his most romantic in the octave, but moving towards his mature style in the sestet.

APPENDIX I

MEMOIR (1931)

by Edmund Blunden

TWELVE years of uneasy peace have passed since the War, among its final victims, took Wilfred Owen, and ten since the choice edition of his poems by his friend Siegfried Sassoon revealed to lovers of poetry and the humanities how great a glory had departed. It is impossible to become deeply acquainted with Owen's work and not to be haunted by comparisons between his genius and his premature death and the wonder and tragedy of his admired Keats. The sense of his promise and achievement has deepened since 1920, and his former editor has been conspicuous among those who have urged the preparation of a new and enlarged volume of Owen's poems, with such biographical notice as can and should be prefixed to them. The reader, who has in his hands a collection of poems by Owen more than twice as extensive as the previous one, will share the present editor's feelings of gratitude to Mrs. Owen and to Mr. Sassoon, who have made the volume possible by the careful preservation and liberal communication of the manuscripts, and whatever documents provided the substance of the memoir. Mrs. Owen, in sending a store of Owen's early notebooks and loose papers for this book, mentions an episode not unfamiliar in the lives of true poets, yet occasioning some natural tears to the devotee of this poet: "He gave me a sack full to burn once, with strict orders 'not to reserve a sheet'. I of course did as he wished—tho' it was like burning my heart."

There survives, however, a quantity of manuscript by Owen, which he had no leisure to organize. Much of it represents the early period of his enthusiasm for poetry, when he was finding his own way to the secrets of style, and discovering the forms of verse on which he would build up his own House Beautiful. These papers are chiefly remarkable as picturing the isolation in which a poet discerns that he is a poet, the delight and difficulty of the high calling to which he finds himself born, and the fruitful uses of practice in thought and its richest verbal presentation. In them, the young Owen is, without knowing it, the guarantor of the eventual poet who, plunged into the abysses of the breaking of nations, has skill to speak. Their fancies, devices, luxuries, concords enabled him to meet the shocks and amazements of immense suffering with the courage of a masterly artist. But I digress too soon and too widely. Early and late, Owen was a productive poet, and that fact, coupled with the fate that denied him opportunity to decide his own poetry, makes the task of editing his manuscripts complicated. Ideas, images, and musical hints rose up in his mind so fast that many of his poems exist in several versions, of which the ultimate 'fair copy' is not to be certainly separated. In reconsidering this problem, and in offering the reader the text and notes before him, I must pay my tribute to the earlier care and insight of Mr. Sassoon, who, it will be remembered, expressed his indebtedness in the preparation of his edition to Miss Edith Sitwell.

Wilfred Owen was born at Plas Wilmot, Oswestry, on March 18, 1893. Another town in which Owen's name is honoured, while the details of his association are scanty, is Birkenhead; and there we know at least the association that he was educated at the Birkenhead Institute. Perhaps, to us who bless him for his poetry, the epoch-making event of his boyhood was a visit to Broxton by the Hill. "Wilfred", his mother informs me, "must have been about ten years old when I took him for a holiday to Broxton"; and a passage that he wrote about ten years after that tells us the rest,

> *For I fared back into my life's arrears*
> *Even the weeks at Broxton, by the Hill,*
> *Where first I felt my boyhood fill*
> *With uncontainable movements; there was born*
> *My poethood.*

Some additional words on his childhood from his mother will be welcomed: "He was always a very thoughtful, imaginative child—not very robust, and never cared for games. As a little child his greatest pleasure was for me to read to him even after he could read himself."

When he was thirteen or fourteen, he showed clearly the fascination that poetry had for him. He was also a passionate acquirer of learning. His choice of acquaintance through life depended on the soundness and value of what he could learn from those he met; as Bacon puts it, "a full man" pleased him. His father twice took him to Brittany between his fourteenth year and his sixteenth; there he seized every chance of conversation with French people, and was discontented only when the time came to return home. He could not have guessed that he should live to cry out, "I shall never again beg father to take me to France!"

In 1911 he matriculated at the London University (he had been a day-student for a short time at University College, Reading, where he attended Botany lectures). By that time he had become (with great diffidence, in fear and trembling almost) a writer of verses, and was deep in the work of Keats and others, but particularly Keats. His own verses of such an early date supply an engaging record of that dominant devotion. Their intrinsic merits are not my object in quoting them. A sonnet, entitled 'Written in a Wood, September 1910', stands thus:

> *Full ninety autumns hath this ancient beech*
> *Helped with its myriad leafy tongues to swell*
> *The dirges of the deep-toned western gale,*
> *And ninety times hath all its power of speech*
> *Been stricken dumb, at sound of winter's yell,*
> *Since Adonais, no more strong and hale,*
> *Might have rejoiced to linger here and teach*
> *His thoughts in sonnets to the listening dell;*
> *Or glide in fancy through those leafy grots*
> *And bird-pavilions hung with arras green,*
> *To hear the sonnets of its minstrel choir.*
> *Ah, ninety times again, when autumn rots,*
> *Shall birds and leaves be mute and all unseen,*
> *⎰Yet shall Keats' voice sing on and never tire.*
> *⎱Yet shall I see fair Keats, and hear his lyre.*

Another sonnet, dated April 21, 1911, was "written at Teignmouth, on a Pilgrimage to Keats's House"; and in it, with imaginative distinction, the young pilgrim speaks his contentment in a day when the sea seemed to share his proud grief for one "whose name was writ on water". In the summer of 1912, Owen followed Keats in a twofold way by writing a poem 'On Seeing a Lock of Keats's Hair', of which this is the final stanza:

> *It is a lock of Adonais' hair!*
> *I dare not look too long; nor try to tell*
> *What glories I see glistening, glistening there.*
> *The unanointed eye cannot perceive their spell.*
> *Turn ye to Adonais; his great spirit seek.*
>   *O hear him; he will speak!*

But this innocent idolatry did not exclude other influences. One warm day in December 1911 he wrote a letter in verse, from somewhere in Oxfordshire.

> *Full springs of Thought around me rise*
> *Like Rivers Four to water my fair garden.*
> *Eastwards, where lie wide woodlands, rich as Arden,*
> *From out the beechen solitudes hath sprung*
> *A stream of verse from aerial Shelley's tongue,*
> *While, as he drifted on between the banks*
> *Of happy Thames, the waters 'neath the planks*
> *Of his light boat gurgled contentedly*
> *And ever with his dreams kept company.*
> *To-day, the music of the slow, turmoiling river,*
> *The music of the rapid vision-giver,*
> *To me are vocal both.*
>   *To eastward, too,*
> *A churchyard sleeps, and one infirm old yew,*
> *Where in the shadows of the fading day,*
> *Musing on faded lives, sate solemn Gray.*
> *There to majestic utterance his soul was wrought,*
> *And still his mighty chant is fraught*
> *With golden teaching for the world, and speaks*
> *Strong things with sweetness unto whoso seeks.*

Yet can I never sit low at his feet
And, questioning, a gracious answer meet.
For he is gone, and his high dignity
Lost in the past (tho' he may haply be
Far in Futurity as well).
            To North
Are hills where Arnold wandered forth
Which, like his verse, still undulate in calm
And tempered beauty.
            And the marriage-psalm
Was sung o'er Tennyson, small space away.

This rhyming letter has something still more intimate, for, towards its close, Owen declares his longing for a new great poet—for all of us, and himself:

Let me attain
To talk with him, and share his confidence.

His loneliness as a young poet breaks out; he may read even Keats and "still", he appeals, "I am alone among the Un- seen Voices".

A serious illness, in 1913, led to his "proceeding to France", as he would have described it a year or two later, with the object of escaping the English winter in its more usual manifestations. He became a tutor at Bordeaux, and remained there long enough to acquire a great deal of the French language—the French way of thinking. At Bordeaux he had the good fortune to become acquainted with that old hero, M. Laurent Tailhade,* the poet, well qualified to spur him on in the delicate yet highly original studies of the poetic art which he was making. Owen was never troubled with doubts whether a poet should be a curious designer of verses or not; he frankly enjoyed the art of verse. He intended, in 1913, to publish 'Minor Poems—in Minor Keys—By a Minor'. Among those, however, I find one of which the

*M. Tailhade wrote, on April 1, 1915: "Votre lettre est charmante. Cette impuissance de vous 'exprimer en français' qui vous fait hésiter, n'existe que dans votre imagination. Vous peignez avec un délicat pinceau; votre piano a les touches nécessaires pour la grâce et l'émotion."

power is so full and the tone so deep and final that Mr. Sassoon, happening upon it in a copy without evidence of date, marks it "Late?" But the poems of the same period are for the most part tentative and without a complete impulse, notwithstanding that some of them are on an ambitious scale. There is an ode on 'The Swift', another on 'Uriconium', and a lengthy tale of the kind that Keats achieved in 'Isabella'— but not from Boccaccio. It is 'The Little Mermaid of Hans Christian Andersen, done into English verse', and extends to seventy-eight stanzas. One of the obvious things about these immature poems is the sensuousness which Owen had in scarcely less degree than even Keats, and the following lines will show it, alike in its command of the unpleasing and the agreeable.

> *A tinge*
> *Curdled the sea, like mingling oil and ink. . . .*
>
> *The witch's den! Around was filthy quag,*
> *In whose soft mire slow-wallowed water-slugs,*
> *Large, fat and white. There sat the fishy hag,*
> *Beneath her hut of bones. . . .*

Of golden hair,

> *This is more like the aureoles of Aurora,*
> *The leaves of flames, the flame of her corona.*
> *Not Petrarch wore such coronals, nor Laura,*
> *Nor yet his orange-trees by old Verona,*
> *Nor gay gold fruits that yellow Barcelona!*

In the possibilities of splendid colours, in the glories of gems and in music of all kinds his spirit expanded. But as yet the perception of life's values which was to be his was lacking to his poetical passion.

Speculating on his future, he expressed his conclusions in May 1914: "I certainly believe I could make a better musician than many who profess to be, and are accepted as such. Mark, I do not for a moment call myself a musician, nor do I suspect I ever shall be, but there! I love Music, with such *strength* that I have had to conceal the passion, for fear it be thought weakness. . . . Failing Music, is it Pictures that I hanker to do? I am not abashed to admit it, but heigh ho! If there were anything in me I should, following Legend, have covered, with spirited fresco, the shed, or carved the staircase knob into a serene Apollo! . . . Let me now seriously and shamelessly work out a Poem."

In July 1914 Owen, like most of his contemporaries, was intent upon the brighter side of experience, and that month he wrote the ingenious and fresh verses beginning

> *Leaves*
> > *Murmuring by myriads in the shimmering trees.*
> *Lives*
> > *Wakening with wonder in the Pyrenees.*
> *Birds*
> > *Cheerily chirping in the early day.*
> *Bards*
> > *Singing of summer scything thro' the hay.*

That note was soon to be changed, and the 'Endymion' phase of Owen's poetical life was at a close. Thenceforward he moved into the sphere of the later 'Hyperion', to the lofty sorrow and threnody of which the latest of his writings must be likened; moreover, when he was to be moved by lighter forces of life, they were to be those of a ghost-like secrecy and dimness. In understanding and expressing those mysterious backwaters of a European war's great current, Owen had the advantage of being attuned to the sadness of the French poets; he is, at moments, an English Verlaine. It did not take him long, after the sudden dismissal of peace, to feel and utter the solemn death of a period, and in himself the transition from a youth of maying to an agedness of mood.

> *Thou hast led me like a heathen sacrifice*
> *With music and with fatal yokes of flowers——*

But he did not display any immediate conception that war was disenchantment, obscenity, and torture. He stood, watching the storm working up, and contemplating the change of empires. He had matured, and was now come to his intellectual stature. He viewed the past, and discerned inevitability.*

In 1915—the date of his enlistment was controlled by his tutorial engagement—he returned to England. He joined the Artists' Rifles. His view of the soldier as the victim began to appear in his verses; he had already written a paradoxical 'Ballad of Purchase Moneys', opening with the aspect of new crusades and modern knightliness, closing with the burden of war.

> *The Sun is sweet on rose and wheat*
> *And on the eyes of children;*
> *Quiet the street for old men's feet*
> *And gardens for the children.*
>
> *The soil is safe, for widow and waif,*
> *And for the soul of England,*
> *Because their bodies men vouchsafe*
> *To save the soul of England.*
>
> *Fair days are yet left for the old,*
> *And children's cheeks are ruddy,*
> *Because the good lads' limbs lie cold*
> *And their brave cheeks are bloody.*

This was the general position; but Owen, like many others in that multitude of unselfish youth, still had moods in which he regarded his individual life as though no devastating force had arrived to baffle its progress. In a long, self-questioning letter of March 5, 1915, he declared his ambitions as those of a poet: "lesser than Macbeth's and greater, not so happy but much happier". Perhaps, as we all did, he clung to the notion that the War would soon be over. "*To be able* to write as *I know how to*, study is necessary: a period of study, then of intercourse with kindred spirits, then of isolation. My heart is ready, but my brain unprepared, and my hand untrained. I quite envisage possibility of non-success."

Gazetted to the Manchester Regiment, Owen joined the

*See *1914*, p. 129.

2nd Battalion in January 1917 on the Somme battlefield, where the last sharp fighting was in progress, in that hardest of winters, before the Germans withdrew to their new trench system. Letters home disclose something of his individual experience and of the general life—now so remote in its singularities—of British infantrymen in Flanders. Before leaving the Base Wilfred wrote: "I have just received Orders to take the train at Étaples, to join the 2nd Manchesters. This is a Regular Regiment, so I have come off mighty well. . . . It is a huge satisfaction to be going among well-trained troops and genuine 'real-old' officers. . . . This morning I was hit! We were bombing, and a fragment from somewhere hit my thumb knuckle. I coaxed out one drop of blood. Alas! no more!! There is a fine heroic feeling about being in France, and I am in perfect spirits. A tinge of excitement is about me, but excitement is always necessary to my happiness." On January 4, he wrote a fuller review of the process which took place between a training-camp and a company in the Line: "I have joined the Regiment, who are just at the end of a six weeks' rest. I will not describe the awful vicissitudes of the journey here. I arrived at Folkestone, and put up at the best hotel. It was a place of luxury—inconceivable now—carpets as deep as the mud here—golden flunkeys; pages who must have been melted into their clothes and expanded since; even the porters had clean hands. Even the dogs that licked up the crumbs had clean teeth. Since I set foot on Calais quays I have not had dry feet. No one knew anything about us on this side, and we might have taken weeks to get here, and *must* have, but for fighting our way here. At the Base, as I said, it was not so bad. We were in the camp of Sir Percy Cunynghame, who had bagged for his Mess the Duke of Connaught's chef. After those two days, we were let down, gently, into the real thing, mud. It has penetrated now into that sanctuary, my sleeping bag, and that holy of holies, my pyjamas. For I sleep on a stone floor, and the servant squashed mud on all my belongings; I suppose by way of baptism. We are 3 officers in this 'Room', the rest of the house is occupied by servants and the band; the roughest set of knaves I have ever been herded with. Even now their language is shaking the flimsy door between the rooms. I chose a servant for myself yesterday, not for his profile, nor yet for clean hands, but for his excellence in bayonet work. For the servant is always at the side of his officer in the charge, and is therefore worth a dozen nurses. Alas, he of the Bayonet is in the Bombing Section, and it is against Regulations to employ such as a servant. I makeshift with another. Everything is makeshift. The English seem to have fallen into the French unhappy-go-lucky non-system. There are scarcely any houses here. The men lie in barns. Our Mess Room is also an Ante and Orderly Room. We eat and drink out of old tins, some of which show traces of ancient enamel. We are never dry, and never 'off duty'. On all the officers' faces there is a harassed look that I have never seen before, and which in England never will be seen—out of jails. The men are just as Bairnsfather has them—expressionless lumps. We feel the weight of them hanging on us. I have found not a few of the old Fleetwood Musketry party here. They seemed glad to see me, as far as the set doggedness of their features would admit. I censored hundreds of letters yesterday, and the hope of peace was in every one. The *Daily Mail* map, which appeared about Jan. 2, will be of extreme interest to you. We were stranded in a certain town one night, and I saved the party of us by collaring an Orderly in the streets and making him take us to a Sergeants' Mess. . . . I am perfectly well and strong, but unthinkably dirty and squalid. I scarcely dare to wash. Pass on as much of this happy news as may interest people. The favourite song of the men is,

> *The Roses round the door*
> *Makes me love mother more.*

They sing this everlastingly. I don't disagree."

Sunday, Jan. 7, 1917. "It is afternoon. We had an Inspection to make from 9 to 12 this morning. I have wandered into a village café where they gave me writing paper. We made a redoubtable march yesterday from the last Camp to this. The awful state of the roads, and the enormous weight carried, was too much for scores of men. Officers also carried full packs, but I had a horse part of the way. It was beginning to freeze through the rain when we arrived at our tents. We were at the mercy of the cold, and, being in health, I never suffered so terribly as yesterday afternoon. I am really quite well, but have sensations kindred to being seriously ill. As I was making my damp bed, I heard the guns for the first time. It was a sound not without a certain sublimity. They woke me again at 4 o'clock. We are two in a tent. I am with the Lewis Gun Officer. We begged stretchers from the doctor to sleep on. Our servant brings our food to us in our tents. This would not be so bad, but for lack of water and the intense damp cold. . . . This morning I have been reading Trench Standing Orders to my platoon (*verb. sap.*). Needless to say I show a cheerier face to them than I wear in writing this letter; but I must not disguise from you the fact that we are at one of the worst parts of the Line. . . . I can't tell you any more Facts. I have no Fancies and no Feelings. Positively they went numb with my feet. Love is not quenched, except the unenduring flickerings thereof." Two days later he reports: "We moved further up yesterday, most of the way on 'buses. I have just had your long-looked-for letter. It seems wrong that ever your dear handwriting should come into such a Gehenna as this. There is a terrific strafe on. The artillery are doing a 48 hours' bombardment. At night it is like a stupendous thunderstorm, for the flashes are quite as bright as lightning. When we arrived at this deserted village last night, there had been no billets prepared for the battalion —owing to misunderstanding. Imagine the confusion! For my part I discovered, or rather my new-chosen and faithful servant discovered, a fine little hut, with a chair in it. A four-leggéd chair! The roof is waterproof, and there is a stove. There is only one slight disadvantage: there is a howitzer just 70 or 80 yards away, firing over the top every minute or so. I can't tell you how glad I am you got me the ear-defenders. I have to wear them at night. Every time No. 2 (the nearest gun) fires, all my pharmacopœia, all my boots, candle, and nerves take a smart jump upwards. This pheno-menon is immediately followed by a fine rain of particles from the roof. I keep blowing them off the page. From time to time the village is shelled, but just now nothing is coming

over. Anyhow there is a good cellar close to. . . . I spent
an hour to-day behind the guns (to get used to them). The
major commanding the battery was very pleasant indeed.
He took me to his H.Q., and gave me a book of poems to
read as if it were the natural thing to do!! But all night I
shall be hearing the fellow's voice:

'Number Two—FIRE!' "

That same afternoon, his next letter mentions, he "took
a tour into the Line which we shall occupy. Our little party
was shelled going up across the open country. It was not at
all frightful, and only one 4.7 got anywhere near, falling
plump in the road, but quite a minute after we had passed the
spot. I tell you these things because *afterwards* they will
sound less exciting. . . . My Company Commander (A
Company) has been out here since the beginning: 'tis a
gentleman *and an original* (!) Next in command is Haydon,
whom I greatly like. . . . Even as they prophesied in the
Artists, I have to take a close interest in feet, and this very
day I knelt down with a candle and watched each man per-
form his anointment with whale oil; praising the clean feet,
but not reviling the unclean. . . . I am not allowed to send
a sketch, but you must know I am transformed now, wearing
a steel helmet, buff-jerkin of leather, rubber-waders up to the
hips, and gauntlets. But for the rifle, we are exactly like
Cromwellian Troopers. The waders are indispensable. In
2½ miles of trench which I waded yesterday there was not
one inch of dry ground. There is a mean depth of 2 feet of
water. . . . These things I need: (1) small pair nail
scissors; (2) celluloid hair-pin box from Boots' with *tight-
fitting lid*, and containing boracic powder; (3) Player's
'Navy Cut'; (4) ink pellets; (5) Sweets (!!). We shall not
be in touch with supplies by day."

This heralded his first trench tour, on the St. Quentin
front. On January 16 he wrote: "I can see no excuse for
deceiving you about these last 4 days. I have suffered
seventh hell. I have not been at the front. I have been in
front of it. I held an advanced post, that is, a 'dug-out' in
the middle of No Man's Land. We had a march of 3 miles

over shelled road, then nearly 3 along a flooded trench. After that we came to where the trenches had been blown flat out and had to go over the top. It was of course dark, too dark, and the ground was not mud, not sloppy mud, but an octopus of sucking clay, 3, 4, and 5 feet deep, relieved only by craters full of water. Men have been known to drown in them. Many stuck in the mud and only got on by leaving their waders, equipment, and in some cases their clothes. High explosives were dropping all around, and machine-guns spluttered every few minutes. But it was so dark that even the German flares did not reveal us. Three-quarters dead, I mean each of us ¾ dead, we reached the dug-out and relieved the wretches therein. I then had to go forth and find another dug-out for a still more advanced post where I left 18 bombers. I was responsible for other posts on the left, but there was a junior officer in charge. My dug-out held 25 men tight packed. Water filled it to a depth of 1 or 2 feet, leaving say 4 feet of air. One entrance had been blown in and blocked. So far, the other remained. The Germans knew we were staying there and decided we shouldn't. Those fifty hours were the agony of my happy life. Every ten minutes on Sunday afternoon seemed an hour. I nearly broke down and let myself drown in the water that was now slowly rising over my knees. Towards 6 o'clock, when, I suppose, you would be going to church, the shelling grew less intense and less accurate; so that I was mercifully helped to do my duty and crawl, wade, climb, and flounder over No Man's Land to visit my other post. It took me half an hour to move about 150 yards. I was chiefly annoyed by our own machine-guns from behind. The seeng-seeng-seeng of the bullets reminded me of Mary's canary. On the whole I can support the canary better. In the platoon on my left the sentries over the dug-out were blown to nothing. One of these poor fellows was my first servant whom I rejected. If I had kept him he would have lived, for servants don't do sentry duty. I kept my own sentries half-way down the stairs during the more terrific bombardment. In spite of this one lad was blown down and, I am afraid, blinded. This was my only casualty. The officer of the left platoon has come out completely prostrated and is in hospital. I am now as well, I suppose, as ever. I allow myself to tell you all these things because *I am never going back to this awful post.* It is the worst the Manchesters have ever held; and we are going back for a rest. I hear that the officer who relieved me left his 3 Lewis guns behind when he came out. (He had only 24 hours in). He will be court-martialled."

Rest, with the infantry on the Western Front, became a term of irony. January 19, 1917: "We are now a long way back, in a ruined village, all huddled together in a farm. We all sleep in the same room where we eat and try to live. My bed is a hammock of rabbit-wire stuck up beside a great shell-hole in the wall. Snow is deep about, and melts through the gaping roof, on to my blanket. We are wretched beyond my previous imagination—but safe. Last night indeed I had to 'go up' with a party. We got lost in the snow. I went on ahead to scout—foolishly alone—and, when half a mile away from the party, got overtaken by

GAS.

It was only tear-gas from a shell, and I got safely back (to the party) in my helmet, with nothing worse than a severe fright! And a few tears, some natural, some unnatural. . . . Coal, water, candles, accommodation, everything is scarce. We have not always air! When I took my helmet off last night—O Air, it was a heavenly thing! . . . They want to call No Man's Land 'England' because we keep supremacy there. It is like the eternal place of gnashing of teeth; the Slough of Despond could be contained in one of its crater-holes; the fires of Sodom and Gomorrah could not light a candle to it—to find the way to Babylon the Fallen. It is pock-marked like a body of foulest disease, and its odour is the breath of cancer. I have not seen any dead. I have done worse. In the dank air I have *perceived* it, and in the darkness, *felt*. Those 'Somme Pictures' are the laughing-stock of the army—like the trenches on exhibition in Kensington. No Man's Land under snow is like the face of the moon, chaotic, crater-ridden, uninhabitable, awful, the abode of madness. To call it 'England'! I would as soon call my House (!)

Krupp Villa, or my child Chlorina-Phosgena. . . . The people of England needn't hope. They must agitate. But they are not yet agitated even. Let them imagine 50 strong men trembling as with ague for 50 hours!"

The winter of 1916–1917 will long be remembered for its scarcely tolerable cold. The 2nd Manchesters did not get the rest expected, and Owen was soon in the front line again. "In this place my platoon had no dug-outs, but had to lie in the snow under the deadly wind. By day it was impossible to stand up, or even crawl about, because we were behind only a little ridge screening us from the Boche's periscope. We had 5 Tommy's Cookers between the platoon, but they did not suffice to melt the ice in the water-cans. So we suffered cruelly from thirst. The marvel is that we did not all die of cold. As a matter of fact, only one of my party actually froze to death before he could be got back, but I am not able to tell how many have ended in hospital. I had no real casualties from shelling, though for 10 minutes every hour whizz-bangs fell a few yards short of us. Showers of soil rained on us but no fragment of shell could find us. . . . My feet ached until they could ache no more, and so they temporarily died. I was kept warm by the ardour of Life within me. I forgot hunger in the hunger for Life. . . . I cannot say I felt any fear. We were all half-crazed by the buffeting of the high explosives. I think the most unpleasant reflection that weighed on me was the impossibility of getting back any wounded, a total impossibility by day, and frightfully difficult by night. We were marooned on a frozen desert. There is not a sign of life on the horizon, and a thousand signs of death. Not a blade of grass, not an insect; once or twice a day the shadow of a big hawk, scenting carrion. By degrees, day by day, we worked back through the reserve and support lines to the crazy village where the Battalion takes breath. While in support we inhabited vast Boche dug-outs (full of all kinds of souvenirs). They are so deep that they seem warm like mines! There we began to thaw. . . . Then I had the heavenly-dictated order to proceed on a Transport Course. Me in Transports? Aren't you?" He was writing from the riding school at Amiens, on February 4, with the prospect of a month's exercise (he was a natural horseman) and lodgings "in a HOUSE". "Quite 10 years ago I made a study of this town and cathedral, in the Treasury. It is all familiar now!" He looked at the "inoffensive sky" and his room, and reflected, "I suppose I can endure cold and fatigue and the face-to-face death as well as another; but extra for me there is the universal pervasion of *Ugliness*. Hideous landscapes, vile noises, foul language, and nothing but foul, even from one's own mouth (for all are devil-ridden) —everything unnatural, broken, blasted; the distortion of the dead, whose unburiable bodies sit outside the dug-outs all day, all night, the most execrable sights on earth. In poetry we call them the most glorious. But to sit with them all day, all night—and a week later to come back and find them still sitting there in motionless groups, THAT is what saps the 'soldierly spirit'."

On March 1 he rejoined his battalion in the extreme south of the British trench line, recently taken over from the French. It was quiet—"so quiet that we have our meals in a shallow dug-out, and only go down deep to sleep". He was soon kept busy in charge of digging parties. On March 14 he reported an accident* of a kind which might easily have been more frequent in the devastated area: "Last night I was going round through pitch darkness to see a man in a dangerous state of exhaustion. I fell into a kind of well, only about 15 ft., but I caught the back of my head on the way down. The doctors (not in consultation!) say I have a slight concussion. Of course I have a vile headache, but I don't feel at all fuddled." Five days later he wrote again of this mishap. "I am in a hospital bed (for the first time in life). After falling into that hole (which I believe was a shell-hole in a floor, laying open a deep cellar) I felt nothing more than a headache, for 3 days; and went up to the front in the usual way—or nearly the usual way, for I felt too weak to wrestle with the mud, and sneaked along the top, snapping my fingers at a clumsy sniper. When I got back I developed a

*It happened at Le Quesnoy-en-Santerre.

high fever, vomited strenuously and long, and was seized with muscular pains. The night before last I was sent to a shanty a bit farther back, and yesterday motored on to this Field Hospital, called Casualty Clearing Station 13." He added that he felt better, and,·on March 21, that he was getting up and expecting soon "to overtake my Battalion" again. However, it was in hospital that he drafted (March 23) the sonnet "With an Identity Disc".

The battalion had been attacking, and he 'caravanned' to them over unfamiliar territory. On the way he had one night's lodging "with a family of refugees, 3 boys, 2 tiny girls: a good class socially, and of great charm personally. I was treated as a god, and indeed begin to suspect I have a heart as comprehensive as Victor Hugo's, Shakspere's, or your own." (He is writing to his mother.) "In 24 hours I never took so many hugs and kisses in my life, no, not in the first chapter even. They took reliefs at it. It would have astounded the English mind." He found his battalion, and was very welcome, for they had not made their successful attack without heavy losses. Then "We stuck to our line 4 days (and 4 nights) without relief, in the open, and in the snow. Not an hour passed without a shell amongst us. I never went off to sleep on those days, because the others were far more fagged after several days of fighting than I fresh from bed. We lay in wet snow. I kept alive on brandy, the fear of death, and the glorious prospect of the cathedral town just below us, glittering with the morning. With glasses I could easily make out the general architecture of the cathedral: so I have told you how near we have got. The French are on the skirts of the town, as I could see. It was unknown where exactly the Boche was lying in front of us. The job of finding out fell upon me. I started out at midnight with 2 corporals and 6 picked men, warning other regiments on our flanks not to make any mistake about us. It was not very long before the Hun sent up his Very lights, but the ground was favourable to us, and I and my corporal prowled on until we clearly heard voices, and the noises of carrying and digging. When I had seen them quite clearly moving about, and marked the line of their entrenchment, it might seem my job was done;

but my orders were to discover the force of the enemy. So then I took an inch or two of cover and made a noise like a platoon. Instantly we had at least two machine-guns turned on us, and a few odd rifles. Then we made a scramble for 'home'. Another night I was putting out an advanced post when we were seen or heard and greeted with shrapnel. The man crouching shoulder to shoulder to me gets a beautiful round hole pierced deep in his biceps. I am nothing so fortunate, being only buffeted in the eyes by the shock and whacked on the calf by a spent fragment, which scarcely tore the puttee."

Almost three weeks passed before his next letter (April 25). He had been in attack in the period. "Never before has the Battalion encountered such intense shelling as rained upon us as we advanced in the open. . . . The reward we got for all this was to remain in the Line 12 days. For twelve days I did not wash my face, nor take off my boots, nor sleep a deep sleep. For twelve days we lay in holes, where at any moment a shell might put us out. I think the worst incident was one wet night when we lay up against a railway embankment. A big shell lit on the top of the bank, just 2 yards from my head. Before I awoke, I was blown in the air right away from the bank! I passed most of the following days in a railway cutting, in a hole just big enough to lie in, and covered with corrugated iron. My brother officer of B Coy., 2nd Lt. G., lay opposite in a similar hole. But he was covered with earth, and no relief will ever relieve him, nor will his Rest be a 9-days-Rest." From this railway cutting it was Owen's duty "about midnight to flounder across to the French and knock at the door of the Company H.Q. and ask if all was well, to be answered by a grunt".

"I think that the terribly long time we stayed unrelieved was unavoidable; yet it makes us feel bitterly towards those in England who might relieve us, and will not. We are now doing what is called a Rest, but we rise at 6.15 and work without break until about 10 P.M., for there is always a Pow-Wow for officers after dinner. And if I have not written yesterday, it is because I must have kept hundreds of letters uncensored, and inquiries about missing men unanswered."

Part of this letter is written on a military document. "I hope", says Owen, "this bit of paper is not incriminating to send over." The document, which recalls the Western Front in a decidedly unpopular aspect, reads:

AMENDMENT
S.S. 143—"INSTRUCTIONS FOR THE TRAINING OF PLATOONS FOR OFFENSIVE ACTION, 1917."

Appendix I.—NOTES—LINE 6. *After* "No. 1" *add* "and No. 2".

On May 2 he wrote from the 13th Casualty Clearing Station: "Here again! The Doctor suddenly was moved to forbid me to go into action next time the Battalion go, which will be in a day or two. I did not go sick or anything, but he is nervous about my nerves, and sent me down yesterday—labelled Neurasthenia. I still of course suffer from the headaches traceable to my concussion. . . . Do not for a moment suppose I have had a 'breakdown'! I am simply avoiding one." Joking over his having escaped actual wounds, he remembers, "I should certainly have got a bullet wound, if I had not used the utmost caution in wriggling along the ground on one occasion. There was a party of Germans in a wood about 200 yards *behind* us, and his trench, which we had just taken, was only a foot deep in places, and I was obliged to keep passing up and down it. As a matter of fact I rather enjoyed the evening after the stunt, being only a few hundred yards from the town, as you knew, and having come through the fire so miraculously, and being, moreover, well fed on the Boche's untouched repast!! It was curious and troubling to pick up his letters where he had left off writing in the middle of a word!"

Owen also sent an account of this attack to a brother who might have illusions of the romance of war (May 14). "The sensations of going over the top are about as exhilarating as those dreams of falling over a precipice, when you see the rocks at the bottom surging up to you. I woke up without being squashed. Some didn't. There was an extraordinary exultation in the act of slowly walking forward, showing ourselves openly. There was no bugle and no drum, for which I was very sorry. I kept up a kind of chanting sing-song:

> *Keep the Line straight!*
> *Not so fast on the left!*
> *Steady on the left!*
> *Not so fast!*

Then we were caught in a tornado of shells. The various 'waves' were all broken up, and we carried on like a crowd moving off a cricket-field. When I looked back and saw the ground all crawling and wormy with wounded bodies, I felt no horror at all, but only an immense exultation at having got through the barrage. We were more than an hour moving over the open, and by the time we came to the German trench every Boche had fled. But a party of them had remained, lying low in a wood close behind us, and they gave us a very bad time for the next four hours. When we were marching along a sunken road, we got the wind up once. We knew we must have passed the German out-posts somewhere on our left rear. All at once the cry rang down, 'Line the bank'. There was a tremendous scurry of fixing bayonets, tugging of breech-covers, and opening pouches, but when we peeped over, behold a solitary German, haring along towards us, with his head down and his arms stretched in front of him, as if he were going to take a high dive through the earth (which I have no doubt he would like to have done). Nobody offered to shoot him, he looked too funny; and that was our only prisoner that day!"

Passing a sunny idleness in scenery which reminded him of the Faerie Queene and of Arthur in Avalon, he nevertheless found himself with a high temperature, and believed he had trench fever. He remained in the Casualty Clearing Station until June 6, when he wrote: "I go down to-day. Where to? Nobody knows. Maybe in the Hospital Train for days."

About June 10, after confused arrangements, Owen was at No. 1 General Hospital. "I think it is very likely that the Americans will send me to England." And a week later he was at the Welsh Hospital, Netley, "in too *receptive* a mood to speak at all about the other side, the seamy side of the

'Manche'. I just wander about absorbing Hampshire."

One of Owen's letters from the hospital on the Somme may be conveniently quoted at this point. It sums up the creed which had taken bold form in his mind, and awaited poetical completion: "Already I have comprehended a light which never will filter into the dogma of any national church: namely, that one of Christ's essential commands was: Passivity at any price! Suffer dishonour and disgrace, but never resort to arms. Be bullied, be outraged, be killed; but do not kill. It may be a chimerical and an ignominious principle, but there it is. It can only be ignored; and I think pulpit professionals are ignoring it very skilfully and successfully indeed. . . . And am I not myself a conscientious objector with a very seared conscience? . . . Christ is literally in 'no man's land'. There men often hear His voice: Greater love hath no man than this, that a man lay down his life for a friend. Is it spoken in English only and French? I do not believe so. Thus you see how pure Christianity will not fit in with pure patriotism."

From Netley, he was sent to what he described on June 26 as "a decayed hydro"—the Craiglockhart War Hospital, a short way out of Edinburgh. "At present", he wrote on August 8, clearly feeling the War's influence even more deeply than before, "I am a sick man in hospital, by night; a poet for quarter of an hour after breakfast; I am whatever and whoever I see while going down to Edinburgh on the train: greengrocer, policeman, shopping lady, errand-boy, paper-boy, blind man, crippled Tommy, bank-clerk, carter, all of these in half an hour; next a German student in earnest; then I either peer over bookstalls, in back-streets, or do a bit of a dash down Princes Street—according as I have taken weak tea or strong coffee for breakfast. . . . Yes, you will like to read Mrs. Browning. Having listened so long to her low, sighing voice (which *can* be *heard* often through the page), and having seen her hair, not in a museum case, but palpably in visions, and having received kindness from a boy to whom she was kind (M. Léger—he is still a boy); for these reasons, I say, the Flapper flaps in vain. The other day I read a biography of Tennyson, which says he was unhappy, even in the midst of his fame, wealth, and domestic serenity. Divine discontent! I can quite believe he never knew happiness for one moment such as I have—for one or two moments. But as for misery, was he ever frozen alive, with dead men for comforters? Did he hear the moaning at the Bar, not at twilight and the evening bell only, but at dawn, noon, and night, eating and sleeping, walking and working, always the close moaning of the Bar; the thunder, the hissing, and the whining of the Bar?—Tennyson, it seems, was always a great child. So should I have been, but for Beaumont Hamel. (Not before January 1917 did I write the *only* lines of mine that carry the stamp of maturity—these:

> *But the old happiness is unreturning,*
> *Boys have no grief as grievous as youth's yearning;*
> *Boys have no sadness sadder than our hope.*)

. . . It is worthy of mention that we have been in mist for 3 days: a gloriously luminous mist at times. I saw Holyrood on Sunday afternoon (being alone on Salisbury Crags), a floating mirage in gold mist; a sight familiar enough in dreams and poems, but which I never thought possible in these islands. It was the picture of a picture. . . ."

At Craiglockhart he was enterprising; he performed at concerts, he lectured, and he edited the hospital magazine called *The Hydra*. About the beginning of August, Captain Siegfried Sassoon arrived. Owen had been reading his *Old Huntsman*. "Nothing like his trench-life sketches has ever been written or ever will be written." One day he ventured to call at his hero's room and to show him some poems, which received some praise and some blame. On the evening of September 7, again, "Sassoon called me in to him; and having condemned some of my poems, amended others, and rejoiced over a few, he read me his very last works, which are superb beyond anything in his book. . . . I don't tell him so, or that I am not worthy to light his pipe. I simply sit tight and tell him where I think he goes wrong." There is a letter of September 22 almost dithyrambic in honour of Mr. Sassoon "as a man, as a friend, and as a poet", and in another Owen refers modestly to "my recent efforts in Sassoon's manner". *The Hydra* was a fortunate periodical; it received new poems by the two best English war-poets. The chance that gave Owen the friendship of Mr. Sassoon, then endeavouring in all ways open to him, but above all by poetical challenge, to shed light on the futile ugliness of the War, was a good one. It supplied the answer to the petition for a poet's companionship which, as has been seen, Owen uttered in his verses years before. To ascribe to it altogether the subsequent self-revelation of Owen as a poet would be incorrect, but the impact of Mr. Sassoon's character, thought, and independent poetic method gave the other a new purpose. Owen might have agreed with the author of *Hudibras*—

> *An English poet should be tried by his peers,*
> *And not by pedants and philosophers,*

—on this occasion. The trial brought out his greatness and directed his passion. With a clear and spacious view of the function of poetry, he rapidly produced the poems which have made him famous.

The problem of dating most of Owen's papers is such that one cannot be sure when he thought out the use of assonances, instead of rhymes, which he perfected. He was, as I have said, an unwearied worker in the laboratory of word, rhythm, and music of language, partly by nature and partly from his close acquaintance with French poetry and its exacting technical subtleties.

Having discovered and practised pararhyme, Owen became aware that it would serve him infinitely in the voicing of emotion and imagination. What he made of it is felt at its fullest, perhaps, in the solemn music of 'Strange Meeting', but again and again by means of it he creates remoteness, darkness, emptiness, shock, echo, the last word. So complete and characteristic is his deployment of this technical resource that imitators have been few; but, indeed, there is another cause why they have been so. Only an innate, unconventional command over language, and a rich and living vocabulary— in short, only a genius for poetry could for long work in that uncommon medium.

The doctor who had charge of Owen at Craiglockhart,

A. Brock, took more than common interest in him, regarding him as "a very outstanding figure, both in intellect and in character". In order to restore his nerves to serenity, Dr. Brock directed his energies to any peaceful pursuit that could be arranged; he proposed to him the writing of a poem on a classical subject, 'Antaeus', put him in touch with the Edinburgh 'submerged tenth', and caused him to give lectures at Tynecastle School. At one time Owen was busy with historical research in the Advocates' Library, at the request of Lord Guthrie, whose great courtesy fascinated him. When, towards the end of October, the question of Owen's transference from Craiglockhart arose imminently, he was unhappy: "I am seriously beginning to have aching sensations at being rooted up from this pleasant Region".

I am indebted to Mrs. Mary Gray, who knew Owen well at this period, for an account of his personality. "The bond which drew us together was an intense pity for suffering humanity—a need to alleviate it, wherever possible, and an inability to shirk the sharing of it, even when this seemed useless. This was the keynote of Wilfred's character; indeed it was, simply, Wilfred. His sensitiveness, his sympathy were so acute, so profound, that direct personal experience and individual development can hardly be said to have existed for him. He could only suffer, or rejoice, vicariously. . . . The objection that he overlooked individual emotion could only be urged by small natures, selfishly engrossed in their woes. To anyone else, it was immediately evident that their troubles and their happiness were his. . . . He was naturally silent, but with a silence more expressive than words. He had a wonderful tenderness. Silent and reserved as he was, he was adored by my little girl of eight months old. He was never, at that time, gay or playful, but he had that tenderness and a wonderful smile—a sort of gentle radiance, and the tacit understanding between him and the child was almost uncanny. It was the same with a large family of very poor children, and their parents. I was interested in an Italian one-eyed street singer with a most tragic history and fine personality. His courage, cheerfulness, and philosophy drew Wilfred to him at once. We went often to their very poor, exquisitely kept home in the slums, where again, despite his silence, gentle gravity, and reserve, Wilfred was adored—there is no other word for it. He suffered deeply from diffidence, and self-distrust. This was entirely unconnected with any consideration of the impression he made on others. He set himself immensely high standards, and in moments of despondency grieved deeply over what he regarded, quite unjustifiably, as his failure to live up to them. Nevertheless, in his most despondent moods he could never be said to have experienced despair. His courage was too indomitable for that, and he never laid down his arms. . . . Throughout this trial he kept alight the spark of divine fire—the steadfast belief that through suffering do we attain to the only true spiritual beauty."

After Craiglockhart, Owen went to Scarborough, and at first, by way of light duty, was appointed major-domo of the hotel where the seventy officers of the 5th (Reserve) Battalion, Manchester Regiment, assembled.

The following excerpts from a letter written by him in November 1917, while they disclose the honour in which he held the recipient, Mr. Sassoon, also give a better impression of Owen's spirit at the time than would be otherwise recoverable. "Know that since mid-September, when you still regarded me as a tiresome little knocker on your door, I held you as Keats + Christ + Elijah + my Colonel + my father-confessor + Amenophis IV. in profile. What's that mathematically? . . . If you consider what the above names have severally done for me, you will know what you are doing. And you have *fixed* my Life—however short. You did not light me: I was always a mad comet; but you have fixed me. I spun round you a satellite for a month, but I shall swing out soon, a dark star in the orbit where you will blaze. It is some consolation to know that Jupiter himself sometimes swims out of ken.

"To come back to our sheep, as the French *never* say, I have had a perfect little note from Robert Ross, and have arranged a meeting at 12.30 on Nov. 9th. He mentioned staying at Half-Moon St., but the house is full.

"I have ordered several copies of *Fairies and Fusiliers*, but shall not buy all, in order to leave the book exposed on the Shrewsbury counters! I'm also getting Colvin's new *Life of Keats*—no price advertised, but, damn it, I'm to enjoy my leave! . . .

"What I most miss in Edinburgh (not Craiglockhart) is the conviviality of the Four Boys (L. *vivere*—to live). Some day I must tell how we sang, shouted, whistled, and danced through the dark lanes through Colinton; and how we laughed till the meteors showered round us, and we fell calm under the winter stars. And some of us saw the pathway of the spirits for the first time. And seeing it so far above us, and feeling the good road so safe beneath us, we praised God with louder whistling; and knew we loved one another as no men love for long.

"Which, if the bridge-players, Craig and Lockhart, could have seen, they would have called down the wrath of Jahveh, and buried us under the fires of the City you wot of."

Following an ancient custom of mankind, he reviewed the past on the last day of 1917, writing thus to his mother: "And so I have come to the true measure of man. I am not dissatisfied [with] my years. Everything has been done in bouts: Bouts of awful labour at Shrewsbury and Bordeaux; bouts of amazing pleasure in the Pyrenees, and play at Craiglockhart; bouts of religion at Dunsden; bouts of horrible danger on the Somme; bouts of poetry always; of your affection always; of sympathy for the oppressed always. I go out of this year a poet, my dear mother, as which I did not enter it. I am held peer by the Georgians; I am a poet's poet. I am started. The tugs have left me; I feel the great swelling of the open sea taking my galleon. Last year, at this time (it is just midnight, and now is the intolerable instant of the Change), last year I lay awake in a windy tent in the middle of a vast, dreadful encampment. It seemed neither France nor England, but a kind of paddock where the beasts are kept a few days before the shambles. I heard the revelling of the Scotch troops, who are now dead, and who knew they would be dead. I thought of this present night, and whether I should indeed—whether we should indeed—whether you would indeed—but I thought neither long nor deeply, for I am a master of elision. But chiefly I thought of the very strange look on all faces in that camp; an incomprehensible look, which a man will never see in England, though wars should be in England; nor can it be seen in any battle. But only in Étaples. It was not despair, or terror, it was more terrible than terror, for it was a blindfold look, and without expression, like a dead rabbit's. It will never be painted, and no actor will ever seize it. And to describe it, I think I must go back and be with them. We are sending seven officers straight out to-morrow. I have not said what I am thinking this night, but next December I will surely do so."

The life that was customarily endured in home camps during 1918 had little (other than mere security) to recommend it, particularly to those who remembered the prevailing good-nature and resourceful activity of the armies in Flanders. Owen wrote to his mother in May 1918, of old associations and of his poetry. "I've been busy this evening with my terrific poem (at present) called 'The Deranged'. This poem the Editor of the *Burlington Magazine*—(a 2/6 Arts Journal which takes no poetry)—old More Adey, I say, solemnly prohibited me from sending to the *English Review*, on the grounds that 'the *English Review* should not be encouraged'!!! Five years ago this would, as you suggest, have turned my head—but nowadays my head turns only in shame away from these first flickers of the limelight. For I am old already for a poet, and so little is yet achieved.

"And I want no limelight, and celebrity is the last infirmity I desire.

"*Fame is the recognition of one's peers.* I have already more than their recognition. . . . Behold, are they not already as many Keatses? As I looked out into the untravelled world over the hedges of Dunsden Garden, I saw them in the dawn and made ready to go out and meet them.

"And they were glad and rejoiced, though I am the gravest and least witty of that grave, witty company."

Among those who had become aware that a new soldier-poet called Owen was arriving, I find the names of Robert Ross, Roderick Meiklejohn, H. W. Massingham, H. G. Wells, Arnold Bennett, and Osbert Sitwell; and Owen was delighted to find himself at last within the circle of men of letters. There was a project of publishing his poems, and William Heinemann, despite "the state of the paper supply", expressed a willingness to undertake it, or at least to consider it. Another author whose acquaintance he made was Charles Scott-Moncrieff, who obtained Owen's criticism and advice for his translation of the 'Song of Roland'. That work was originally dedicated 'To Mr. W. O.', with a tribute to his mastery of the art of poetry; when it was published in 1919, it contained instead a group of poems in memory of three friends, one of which is a sonnet to Owen:

In the centuries of time to come
Men shall be happy and rehearse thy fame.

Scott-Moncrieff, then at the War Office, endeavoured to find some post for Owen which would mean that he would be kept in England. On May 21, Owen had some prospect "of becoming Instructing Staff Officer to a Cadet Battalion. I would *rather*," he wrote, "work in the War Office itself, and that seems not impossible either. Really I would *like most* to go to Egypt or Italy, but that is not entertained by Scott-Moncrieff." In the end, none of these plans or wishes materialized.

At the close of July he was preparing to go overseas. "Now must I throw my little candle on [Sassoon's] torch and go out again. There are rumours of a large draft of officers shortly." A few days later he reported that he was to attend for medical inspection, and would proceed to France. "I am glad. That is I am much gladder to be going out again than afraid. I shall be better able to cry my outcry, playing my part. The secondary annoyances and discomforts of France behind the line can be no worse than this Battalion. On Friday we were called up at 3 A.M. and had the usual day's work. The Adjutant is ill, and Stiebel is ill. I did Stiebel's job on the stunt, and am still doing it. There are only mock alarms of course. But this morning at 8.20 we heard a boat torpedoed in the bay, about a mile out, they say who saw it. I think only 10 lives were saved. I wish the Boche would have the pluck to come right in and make a clean sweep of the pleasure boats, and the promenaders on the Spa, and all the stinking Leeds and Bradford war-profiteers now reading *John Bull* on Scarborough Sands."

Other letters carry Owen's story towards its untimely close. There was a last day with his mother. Looking with her across the Channel, he repeated a favourite passage from Rabindranath Tagore: "When I go from hence, let this be my parting word, that what I have seen is unsurpassable". On August 31, 1918, he reported his embarkation to Mr. Sassoon: "I have been incoherent ever since I tried to say good-bye on the steps of Lancaster Gate. But everything is clear now; and I'm in hasty retreat towards the Front. Battle is easier here; and therefore you will stay and endure old men and women to the End, and wage the bitterer war and more hopeless." Another message followed quickly: "The sun is warm, the sky is clear, the waves are dancing fast and bright. But these are not Lines written in Dejection. Serenity Shelley never dreamed of crowns me. Will it last when I shall have gone into Caverns and Abysmals such as he never reserved for his worst daemons? . . . And now I am among the herds again, a Herdsman; and a Shepherd of sheep that do not know my voice." Such was, indeed, the feeling of a young officer with temporary hundreds of men suddenly entrusted to him for marching somewhere or other at the base. But Owen was quickly with his old battalion, and he obtained the command of D Company. His new experiences, as he had anticipated, were terrible, but he maintained the serenity of which he spoke, and he continued to write poems on the war. He wrote to Mr. Sassoon on September 22: "You said it would be a good thing for my poetry if I went back. That is my consolation for feeling a fool. This is what shells scream at me every time: 'Haven't you got the wits to keep out of this?'" And on October 10: "Your letter reached me at the exact moment it was most needed—when we had come far enough out of the line to feel the misery of billets; and I had been seized with writer's cramp after making out my casualty reports. (I'm O.C. D Coy.) The Battalion had a sheer time last week. I can find no better epithet; because I cannot say I suffered anything, having let my brain grow dull. That is to say, my nerves are in perfect order.

"It is a strange truth: that your *Counter-Attack* frightened me much more than the real one: though the boy by my side, shot through the head, lay on top of me, soaking my shoulder, for half an hour.

"Catalogue? Photograph? Can you photograph the crimson-hot iron as it cools from the smelting? That is what Jones's blood looked like, and felt like. My senses are charred.

"I shall feel again as soon as I dare, but now I must not. I don't take the cigarette out of my mouth when I write Deceased over their letters.

"But one day I will write Deceased over many books.

"I am glad I've been recommended for M.C., and hope I get it, for the confidence it may give me at home. Full of confidence after having taken a few machine-guns* (with the help of one seraphic lance-corporal), I held a most glorious brief peace talk in a pill-box. You would have been *en pâmoisons*." His Military Cross was duly awarded.

I quote further from the letter of October 10, 1918: "Yes, there is something you can send me: 2 copies of *Counter-Attack*, one inscribed. One is for the Adjutant—who begged a book of Erskine MacD.'s *Soldier-Poets* which I had with me—because I met one of these amalgamations at the Base. And liked him for his immediate subjugation to my principles and your mastery. . . . At the Base I met O'Riordan (of the Irish Theatre, and collaborator with Conrad). A troll of a man; not unlike Robbie (Ross) for unexpected shocks. It was easy, and, as I reflect, inevitable, to tell him everything about oneself. . . . While you are apparently given over to wrens, I have found brave companionship in a poppy, behind whose stalk I took cover from five machine-guns and several howitzers. I desire no more *exposed flanks* of any sort for a long time.

"Of many who promised to send me literary magazines no one has succeeded, except the Editor of *To-day*. . . ."†

*"I only shot one man with my revolver (at about thirty yards!); the others I took with a smile."

†Holbrook Jackson.

A fellow officer, Lieut. J. Foulkes, M.C., has obligingly written down his reminiscences of the Owen who belonged to the trenches and billets of Flanders. "We travelled together (in company with Major Murphy, D.S.O., who was to become 2nd in Command, and, in early November, commanded the 2nd Manchesters) from the base, Étaples, to meet the Battalion at Corbie on the R. Ancre. . . . The first real attack in which we took part was the one which followed the capture of the Hindenburg Line. We had to take what I think was then looked upon as a 2nd Hindenburg Line and which I remember was well wired. The attack was successful but costly—Owen and I were the only officers left in our Company and he became *pro tem.* Company Commander. It was for his work here that he received the M.C. Left with few men and lacking any means of cover save a German pill-box, which was really a death-trap because it was on this that the enemy concentrated his fire, Owen succeeded in holding the line until relieved by the Lancs. Fusiliers some time afterwards. This is where I admired his work—in leading his remnants, in the middle of the night, back to safety. I remember feeling how glad I was that it was not my job to know how to get out. I was content to follow him with the utmost confidence in his leadership."

On October 29 he wrote, during the advance: "The civilians here are a wretched, dirty, crawling community, afraid of *us*, some of them, and no wonder, after the shelling we gave them three weeks ago. Did I tell you that five healthy girls died of fright in one night at the last village? The people in England and France who thwarted a peaceable retirement of the enemy from these areas are therefore now sacrificing aged French peasants and charming French children to our guns. Shells made by women in Birmingham are at this moment burying little children alive not very far from here. It is rumoured that Austria has really surrendered. The new soldiers cheer when they hear these rumours, but the old ones bite their pipes, and go on cleaning their rifles, unbelieving." On October 31 he described his company headquarters as "The Smoky Cellar of the Forester's House", and insisted on the happiness that he felt there, though "so thick is the smoke that I can hardly see by a candle 12 inches away, and so thick are the inmates that I can hardly write for pokes, nudges, and jolts."

Writing to his mother, Owen repeated the words, "My nerves are in perfect order . . . I came out," he added, "in order to help these boys—directly by leading them as well as an officer can, indirectly by watching their sufferings that I may speak of them as well as a pleader can. I have done the first." He had, and he was to continue to the end, which came one week before the Armistice fell from heaven on those colourless and water-logged battle-fields. On November 4, 1918, in face of those resolute German machine-gunners who would not have yielded yet if they could have helped it, Wilfred Owen was endeavouring to pass his company over the Sambre Canal. "Zero," writes Mr. Foulkes, "was, I think, 6 A.M., and once more our Company was to lead. From the 'kicking-off trench' or road we reached the spot on the Canal which should have been temporarily bridged by the Engineers, but the plan had unfortunately failed owing to the heavy fire concentrated by machine-gunners and artillery at that particular spot. Instead of gaining the other side, we had therefore to take cover behind the Canal bank, which rose to a height of about four feet. Attempts were made to cross on rafts, but these were unsuccessful." Owen is remembered patting his men on the back as he moved about, with a "Well done!" and "You are doing very well, my boy". The Engineers who were trying to bridge the Canal almost all became casualties. Owen took a hand with some duckboards or planks, and was at the water's edge helping his men to fix them when he was hit and killed. "The battalion eventually crossed lower down by means of a bridge near the village of Ors, a few miles south of Landrécies."

The indirect part of his sacrifice was then, for a brief moment, unnecessary. Peace came, men returned home, it seemed as though all the bugles in the world might blow without ever luring one of them again into the battle. But in a short time it was apparent that the peace was imperfect, and her olive-branch might easily turn into a rifle-grenade. We are not yet sure of ourselves. A threat hangs over us even now. The transmutation even of the European tragedy into a lending-library fashion shows anew how easy it is for humanity to follow a dream, and how hard it is for the romantic *Homo sapiens*—the *Homo rapiens* of Mr. H. S. Salt—to be a realist. In the coming race there will be a multitude of mirage-builders, and the business which now engages the heart and brain of so many leaders in every country is how to save them from the normal consequences of their own illusions, or those who, for whatever purpose, encourage and exploit them. Here Owen will be found achieving his object of pleading; being dead he speaks. He speaks as a soldier, with perfect and certain knowledge of war at grips with the soldier; as a mind, surveying the whole process of wasted spirit, art, and blood in all its instant and deeper evils; as a poet, giving his readers picture and tone that whenever they are reconsidered afford a fresh profundity, for they are combinations of profound recognitions.

He was, apart from Mr. Sassoon, the greatest of the English war poets. But the term 'war poets' is rather convenient than accurate. Wilfred Owen was a poet without classifications of war and peace. Had he lived, his humanity would have continued to encounter great and moving themes, the painful sometimes, sometimes the beautiful, and his art would have matched his vision. He was one of those destined beings who, without pride of self (the words of Shelley will never be excelled), "see, as from a tower, the end of all". Outwardly, he was quiet,* unobtrusive, full of good sense; inwardly, he could not help regarding the world with the dignity of a seer.

Owen was preparing himself to the last moment in experience, observation, and composition for a volume of poems, to strike at the conscience of England in regard to the con-

*"My impression was that nobody knew he was a poet. Save for some snatches of conversation between him and Captain Somerville, M.C., company commander in Corbie in September 1918, in which the names Sassoon, *Nation*, *Athenæum* were mentioned, I personally never dreamt of it." (Lieut. Foulkes)

tinuance of the war. This volume had begun to take a definite form in his mind, which may be traced in the hastily written and obscurely amended Preface and Contents found among his papers. That they and his later poems exist at all in writing is, to all who knew, or realize, the fierce demands made on company officers in the front line and in its vicinity, a wonderful proof of his intellectual determination.

APPENDIX TWO

Wild with All Regrets

My arms have mutinied against me,—brutes!
My fingers fidget like ten idle brats,
My back's been stiff for hours, damned hours.
Death never gives his squad a Stand-at-ease.
I can't read. There: it's no use. Take your book.
A short life and a merry one, my buck!
We said we'd hate to grow dead-old. But now,
Not to live old seems awful: not to renew
My boyhood with my boys, and teach 'em hitting,
Shooting and hunting,—all the arts of hurting!
—Well, that's what I learnt. That, and making money.
Your fifty years in store seem none too many,
But I've five minutes. God! For just two years
To help myself to this good air of yours!
One Spring! Is one too hard to spare? Too long?
Spring air would find its own way to my lung,
And grow me legs as quick as lilac-shoots.

*   *   *

Yes, there's the orderly. He'll change the sheets
When I'm lugged out. Oh, couldn't I do that?
Here in this coffin of a bed, I've thought
I'd like to kneel and sweep his floors for ever,—
And ask no nights off when the bustle's over,
For I'd enjoy the dirt. Who's prejudiced
Against a grimed hand when his own's quite dust,—
Less live than specks that in the sun-shafts turn?
Dear dust—in rooms, on roads, on faces' tan!
I'd love to be a sweep's boy, black as Town;
Yes, or a muck-man. Must I be his load?
A flea would do. If one chap wasn't bloody,
On went stone-cold, I'd find another body.

*   *   *

Which I shan't manage now. Unless it's yours.
I shall stay in you, friend, for some few hours.
You'll feel my heavy spirit chill your chest,
And climb your throat on sobs, until it's chased
On sighs, and wiped from off your lips by wind.

I think on your rich breathing, brother, I'll be weaned
To do without what blood remained me from my wound.

December 5, 1917.

BM has one draft, with dedication *To S.S.* and a footnote *May I?*
HO has one early draft and two part-drafts.

Anthem for Dead Youth.

What passing bells for these who die so fast?
— Only the monstrous anger of the guns.
Let the majestic insults of their mouths
Be as the priest-words of their requiem.
Of choristers and holy music, none;
Nor any voice of mourning, save the wail
The long-drawn wail of high far-sailing shells.

What candles may we hold for these lost souls?
— Not in the hands of boys, but in their eyes
Shall many candles shine, and will light them.
And Women's wide-spreaded arms shall be their wreaths,
And pallor of girls' cheeks shall be their palls.
Their flowers, the tenderness of mortal minds,
And every Dusk, a drawing-down of blinds.

First Draft
(With Sassoon's amendments.)

First Draft of *Anthem for Doomed Youth*

Anthem for Dead Youth.

What passing-bells for you who die in herds?
— Only the monstrous anger of the more guns!
— Only the stuttering rifles' rattled words
Can patter out your hasty orisons.
No chants for you, nor balms, nor wreaths, nor bells,   choirs
    Nor any voice of mourning, save the choirs,   shells
And, long-drawn sighs
The shall demented choirs of wailing shells;
    And bugles calling for you from sad shires.

What candles may we hold to speed you all?
    Not in the hands of boys, but in their eyes
Shall shine the holy lights [of long goodbyes.
The pallor of girls' brows shall be your pall; comrades'
Your flowers, the tenderness of mortal minds,
And each slow dusk, a drawing down of blinds.

                              Wilfred Owen.

Second Draft

What passing-bells for these for dumb-dying cattle?
  — Only the monstrous anger of more guns!
Only the stuttering rifles' rapid rattle
  Can patter out their hasty orisons.
No chants for them, nor wreaths, nor asphodels,
  Nor any voice of mourning save the choirs
The shrill demented choirs of wailing shells;
  And bugles calling for them from sad shires.

What candles may we hold to speed them all?
  Not in the hands of boys, but in their eyes
Shall shine the holy gleams of their goodbyes.
  The pallor of girls' cheeks shall be their pall.
Their flowers the tenderness of silent minds
And each slow dusk a drawing-down of blinds.

Third Draft

Anthem for ~~Dead~~ Youth —   Nation

What passing-bells for these who die as cattle?
  — Only the monstrous anger of the guns.
    Only the stuttering rifles' rapid rattle
Can patter out their hasty orisons.
No ~~mockeries~~ for them; ~~from~~ prayers nor bells;
  Nor any voice of mourning save the choirs,—
The shrill, ~~demented~~ choirs of wailing shells;
And bugles calling for them from sad shires.

What candles may be held to speed them all?
  Not in the hands of boys, but in their eyes
Shall shine the holy glimmers of goodbyes.
And The pallor of girls' brows shall be their pall;
  Their flowers the tenderness of ~~silent patient~~ minds,
And each slow dusk a drawing-down of blinds.

(These words were written by
S.S. when W. showed him the
sonnet at Craiglockhart in
Sept. 1917.)

Final Draft

INDEX OF FIRST LINES

So Abram rose, and clave the wood, and went   42
Sojourning through a southern realm in youth   132
So neck to stubborn neck, and obstinate knee to knee   120
So the church Christ was hit and buried   83
Suddenly night crushed out the day and hurled   90
Sweet is your antique body, not yet young   99

The beautiful, the fair, the elegant   140
The browns, the olives, and the yellows died   103
The imbecile with long light hair, so light   139
There was a whispering in my hearth   91
The roads also have their wistful rest   96
They watch me, those informers to the Fates   122
This is the track my life is setting on   123
Though unseen Poets, many and many a time   119
Three rompers run together, hand in hand   137

Under his helmet, up against his pack   57

Vividly gloomy, with bright darkling glows   135

War broke: and now the winter of the world   129
We'd found an old Boche dug-out, and he knew   61
What passing-bells for those who die as cattle?   44
When I awoke, the glancing day looked gay   121
Who are these? Why sit they here in twilight?   69
With B.E.F. June 10. Dear Wife   60

"You! What d'you mean by this?" I rapped   79